CHRISTIAN PARALLELS

Working Towards Spiritual Maturity
Through the Medium of Skiing

Trevor Rhoderick Summerlin

**Kingdom
Publishers**

ISBN: 978-1-913247-61-4

1st Edition by Kingdom Publishers Kingdom
Publishers London, UK.

You can purchase copies of this book from
any leading bookstore or email
contact@kingdompublishers.co.uk

Contents

This book will help you improve your walk with God and, although you don't have to be a skier to read it, you may be motivated to book a ski holiday after you've read it !

All colour photographs were supplied by Getty Images UK.
All black and white pictures were provided by Shutterstock UK.

All references, unless otherwise stated are taken from
The New International Version of The Bible (NIV).

Foreword

My mother was a wonderful Christian lady but she did have her idiosyncrasies, for instance, she always read the last chapter of a novel first. When I asked her why, she replied, "Because I like to know how it is going to end; I can take all the ups and downs of the plot if I know it ends well". I have adopted this strange practise, so this is how Trevor sums up this book;

"The Christian, just like the skier, is going to encounter different challenges every day and so maturity must be a constantly developing quality. It is not something that once acquired, remains static or permanent, but instead requires constant attention and spiritual growth to continue to be relevant. What may have seemed a mature response yesterday may not be relevant at all today. So we need to be careful not to fall into using the same approaches, techniques or words that may have worked in the past. This leads towards a ritualistic approach and shows a distinct lack of maturity.

There is no formula in Christian maturity; it is all about our personal relationship with Jesus."

The book will be of special interest to skiers and Christians who want to grow in grace and in the knowledge of our Lord Jesus Christ. Trevor knows about both skiing and Christian discipleship and has excelled at and taught both.

Nothing is more central to the Christian faith than the Good News of God's love and desire to make disciples. Trevor points out in this book the absolute necessity of putting our trust in the Lord Jesus to save us and then going on to Christian maturity in the power and enabling of the Holy Spirit. It is warmly illustrated with personal anecdotes, photographs and sketches of skiers in action, stories from the lives of great Christians, hymns and choruses of the Christian faith and powerful biblical examples.

This very readable book is a distillation of Trevor's many years of Ministry and as a Skiing instructor, and is a crystallization of the biblical truth that has shaped his thinking and empowered his life.

It is said that you have to live with a person to really know them. Should that be true, then I am well qualified to write this foreword for in the late 1960's Trevor moved to live with our family for a year, and has for the last 50 years been a part of our extended family and my friend and confidant.

It is a privilege to be identified with this book because Trevor and I share a passion for making Jesus known and making disciples of those who follow Jesus. As you read this book, anticipate a fresh, new examination of every area of your walk with God and may it lead to you becoming a better skier and importantly, more like the Lord Jesus Christ.

Rev. JOHN JAMES, Penarth
(President of The Baptist Union of Great Britain 1996/7)

Acknowledgements

I am especially grateful to Ian Mayo, head of Oak Hall Holidays, to Bob Fleming who was the Managing Director of MasterSki Holidays, and to Ben Turner who was the founder of Richmond Holidays. They all generously allowed me to be involved both in ski instruction and Bible teaching on so many of their Christian holiday programmes. I am also profoundly grateful to all the members of the teams I worked alongside and to the vast number of guests who were instrumental, often without realising it, in the development of these ideas.

I am extremely grateful also for the excellent teaching, training and coaching I received from John Shedden, the English Ski Council Director of Coaching, and from Stuart Adamson and Alan Hole who were my BASI trainers. My thanks also go to my personal mentor and life-long friend, Rev John C. James, from whom I have learned so much about the practicalities of living the Christian life.

Any use of the words 'he', 'his', 'her' or 'hers' are not meant to imply any gender preference but are intended as totally inclusive terms.

Photographs

All colour photographs have been supplied by Getty Images UK. with the exception of No. 13 – the author.

The black and white pictures throughout the text have been supplied under licence from Shutterstock UK.

Introduction

This book draws on my experience as an internationally qualified Ski Instructor and Coach and my time as a Baptist Pastor and Bible teacher. I have tried to look at each aspect of downhill skiing in order to see what comparisons, or parallels, can be made with a person's journey towards maturity in the Christian life. I have attempted to use a similar system to the one Jesus used to get His message across, by taking the everyday things people could encounter in the skiing world and then applying the 'parable' principle to them.

My time, both as a Baptist minister and a Christian counsellor, have enabled me to identify lots of similarities in the challenges and obstacles that people can face on their Christian journey. I therefore include many personal observations and assessments of how people might benefit from facing and dealing with these sorts of issues.

I hope this book will encourage the avoidance of any form of complacency as people seek to move forward in the Christian life and that it will help them look beyond what they can see merely in the physical dimension. We are, after all, spiritual beings, although for the moment, we live in a physical body and relate to the world around us, primarily, through our physical senses.

The book begins by assessing how essential it is for each person to develop a completely different approach to the way they see themselves, and everything around them. It then goes on to look at the various elements that contribute to a person's experience as they progress into the world of skiing, including the development of specific skiing skills. No aspect is avoided and each one is seen as having something from which lessons can be learned on the journey towards spiritual maturity.

"Maximise your potential to grow into Christian maturity"

Christian Parallels | PART 1

What is it about Skiing and Christianity ?

Who would have thought there could be so many similarities between skiing and the Christian life? What images do each of these conjure for us? Many people might think that the one appears to be for extrovert, sporty, young, fashionable, full-of-life, outdoor people and the other seems to appeal mainly to old, traditional, set-in-their-ways people. In reality, nothing could be further from the truth because both sets of people have embarked on a journey which they hope will be filled with adventure and excitement as they begin their quest to achieve a level of maturity and competence.

I became totally hooked on skiing from the very first opportunity that was presented to me, even though I started comparatively late in life – my twenties ! By this time I had already developed as a teacher and a trainer, and so it seemed natural for me to have an in-built desire to want to qualify eventually as a ski instructor. Although this took me a further ten years, I have sought, in this book, to take advantage of many of the experiences I went through on that journey. There are a number of different disciplines in skiing but I have concentrated solely on the one I was drawn to initially – the discipline known as downhill skiing.

SIMILARITIES

As I reflected on the many and varied aspects of my journey in downhill skiing I have discovered that there are some incredible similarities between this and my journey in the Christian life. For a person learning to ski, the art of being able to turn both skis at the same time in smooth and graceful arcs (parallel turns) is generally seen as the pinnacle of achievement because it opens a whole new realm of freedom and exhilaration. For many people however, this can create unnecessary pressure which is always just out of reach and can rob them of their enjoyment. A comparable challenge here for a developing Christian, might be to live and move in the supernatural power of The Holy Spirit on a daily basis. Once again, this can represent, for some people, an equally unattainable prospect. Therefore, for the purposes of this book, I define the reaching of each of these positions as having acquired a level of maturity and competence. By maturity and competence, I mean the ability to handle all kinds of circumstances or situations as they arise, without being fazed by any of them. Both as a skier and as a Christian, I want to encourage people to move on from the basic skills and grow into a level of genuine maturity (Hebrews 6 v 1 - 3). I am aware that for this to happen, it is vital for some basic principles to be accurately established at an early stage. This will help to ensure that future progress is not restricted or thrown off course in any way. To facilitate this, I want to compare and contrast these two great passions of mine in the sincere hope that this will prompt many people to want to explore each of these in more depth for themselves.

A skier performing parallel turns down a steep slope

MEMORIES

I well remember as a child being fascinated by beautiful pictures of the snow covered mountains of Switzerland and would often cut them out of magazines to keep whenever I could. The first opportunity I had to visit Switzerland was on a school educational expedition to the Bernese Oberland when I was 14 years old. What is heavily imprinted on my mind about that trip is that the educational element had to be severely restricted because of a massive snowfall immediately prior to our arrival. As schoolboys, we were of course, absolutely overjoyed by this and were able to spend lots of time tobogganing on the nearby hills instead of making long treks to view hanging valleys and the like. I didn't realise it then, but it was to be another 15 years before I would return to Switzerland as a skier and be able to really appreciate and enjoy some of the most beautiful ski resorts in the world.

I have always loved snow and have fond memories of building snowmen in our tiny back garden in Catharine Street, Cambridge, where I grew up. Whenever there was a snowfall I would enjoy frequent snowball fights with the other kids in our street and we would often challenge each other in snow clearing races up and down the street until it was too dark to see. One activity which always captivated us was making a long slide. We did this by continually running at, and then skidding over a small patch of snow so that it became compressed and icy. I think this was the precursor to snowboarding !

It was during the great 'freeze' of 1963 that I first saw the sea frozen. My parents had taken me to visit an aunt in Hunstanton and I have vivid memories of staring in awe and amazement at the static sea and marvelling at how whole trees had been covered with such a thick hoar frost that every twig and branch was highlighted in white. The river Cam was frozen solid that year and I was able to witness cars being driven along it by some university students. This prompted my mother to dig out her ice skates and persuade me to give this a try. Her father had in the past competed in the 'Champion of the Fens' ice skating races so it seemed that there just might have been a winter sports gene in my family.

LEARNING TO SKI

My actual introduction to skiing began while I was working for an outdoor activity company which specialised in Camping, Climbing, Canoeing, Caving and Skiing. An important part of the company was a large retail outlet where we sold all the clothing and equipment needed for these activities and, as ways of developing interest and sales in the ski clothing and equipment, we were offering introductory courses in 'Pre-ski exercises and techniques' and provided maintenance and repair services for people's skis. At this time the ski industry in Britain was growing rapidly so, in order to continue to expand our services, it was decided that I should get some formal skiing training. The company sent me on a course to the Scottish National Outdoor Training Centre at Glenmore Lodge, near Aviemore, to learn to ski and to understand all about the technicalities of maintaining the equipment. As I reflect on this now, I can see that this became a major turning point in my life.

The Glenmore Lodge training programme was very comprehensive and quite intense and, after what seemed like ages of static instruction and acclimatisation, the excitement of actually sliding on skis was, for me, electrifying. I loved it. Being able to literally whizz along over the snow on quite gentle gradients of the beginners slopes was just so much fun – I never wanted it to stop. The necessary additional learning about the construction of skis and how to adjust and maintain ski bindings was awfully dull in comparison, nevertheless, I thoroughly enjoyed every minute of my time there and came back totally fired up about the sport. The quality of the instruction was so good and the atmosphere at the centre was so infectious that I chose to visit the centre several more times over the next few years and developed a strong affection for the Cairngorms and the work of the centre.

WORK IN THE SKI INDUSTRY

Throughout my time at the Outdoor Activity Centre I had been able to build connections with a group of local people who, like me, were hooked on skiing. Eventually I was appointed as the General Manager of the centre and got involved in the development of a nearby artificial ski slope. We formed a club and I served as its chairman for 3 years during which time we completely upgraded and re-surfaced the slope, installed a drag lift, put up floodlighting, purchased a club hut, filled it with equipment which could be hired out, developed a team of instructors at different levels, ran regular ski training courses and organised trips and holidays to the snow for the enthusiasts.

In my early days at the Outdoor Activity Centre I had qualified under the National Ski Federation of Great Britain (NSFGB) as an Artificial Slope Ski Instructor (ASSI). However, since I was keen to obtain a snow qualification I soon progressed onto the training courses of the British Association of Ski Instructors (as it was then called), and eventually qualified as a BASI Instructor. Later I was accepted as a Professional Ski Instructor of America (PSIA) and qualified as a Skiing Coach with the English Ski Council.

PROMOTING SKIING

Eventually I moved on from the activity centre and was appointed to a marketing and development role for Dendix Ski Slopes, a company manufacturing an artificial uPVC surface for skiing - the world leader in its field at that time. I was initially involved in the development and marketing of their products and services throughout the UK, but later had responsibility for marketing across Europe, then in the USA and eventually in many nations where skiing was recognised around the world. During this time I pioneered the development of the British Ski Slope Operators Association, started the UK Ski Consultancy Panel, and was Vice President of The English Ski Council for three years. Strangely enough, my busiest times were always throughout the summer when all the ski slope maintenance and extensions were taking place and new slopes were being developed. It meant that I was able to take all my holiday in the (quieter) winter months so that I could spend the maximum amount of time skiing and teaching on the snow.

As a ski instructor and a Christian I have always been thrilled to be able to work, not just on artificial slopes around the UK, but in the stunningly beautiful scenery of snow covered mountains, and this has dramatically increased my appreciation of this aspect of God's creation. The idea of writing a book about this became firmly fixed in my mind one day, when I spotted a huge poster that filled a ski shop window proclaiming "In 6 days God made heaven and earth – and on the 7th day He went skiing" ! This prompted me to begin to make links in my mind between every aspect of skiing and various elements of the Christian life. My enthusiasm and enjoyment of this 'parable game' continued to develop over the years with my involvement in several Christian holiday companies, with whom I was able to work as both a ski instructor and a Bible teacher. I am most grateful to the owners and directors of Oak Hall, MasterSki and Richmond Holidays, for allowing me so many opportunities. Over many years I completed more than 60 skiing trips in total with these companies and was able to teach and minister to hundreds of people who were at very different stages of both their faith and their skiing journeys.

CHRISTIAN CALLING

After working in the ski industry for over twenty years, I was called into The Ministry, as a Baptist Pastor. This enabled me to enjoy studying things from a completely different perspective. I marvelled at how so many principles of the Christian life, as recorded in The Bible, seem to have a direct parallel with some aspect of skiing and I loved being able to use the practical aspects of skiing as illustrations to help people explore and understand more of The Bible. God has given us The Bible as His manual for life. He sets out for us how we might get the very best out of our time on this earth and what we need to do to move towards spiritual maturity.

In the apostle Paul's letter to the Ephesians, which is recognised as the definitive Biblical work regarding the development and make-up of The Body of Christ – the church, Paul makes it clear that the church can only grow and fulfil its God-given role in society as its individual members develop and mature in their personal relationship with Jesus. We recognise that spiritual maturity has absolutely nothing to do with age, education or experience, but it is our ability and willingness to accept that God has higher plans and purposes in every situation than those we are generally able to perceive. We can see how God is constantly trying to encourage us to recognise that we are not on this earth merely for our own benefit but that we have been designed to be 'glory carriers' who bring praise and honour to Him in everything we do (1 Corinthians 10 v 31).

However, the real struggle in the Christian life is to work at bringing every facet of our lives into line with God so that we can continue to grow (mature) in the faith (Ephesians 4 v 13). This is summed up beautifully in the words of the following hymn:

> Take my life and let it be,
> Consecrated, Lord to Thee,
> Take my moments and my days,
> Let them flow in ceaseless praise.
> Take my hands and let them move,
> At the impulse of Your love,
> Take my feet and let them be,
> Swift and beautiful for Thee.
> Take my voice and let me sing,
> Always, only, for my King,
> Take my lips and let them be,
> Filled with messages from Thee.
> Take my silver and my gold,
> Not a mite would I withhold,
> Take my intellect and use,
> Every power as Thou shalt choose.
> Take my will and make it Thine,

It shall be no longer mine,
Take my heart, it is Thine own,
It shall be Your royal throne.
Take my love, my Lord I pour,
At Thy feet its treasure store,
Take myself and I will be,
Ever only, all for Thee.

Frances Ridley Havergal (1836 - 1879)

As we grow closer to Him we automatically grow closer to one another and it is only then that we begin to see the true pattern of His Body emerging - a Body working, performing and growing in complete peace and harmony. This principle is perfectly demonstrated as you watch an accomplished skier appearing to glide effortlessly across varying snow conditions, down a mixture of gradients and around a variety of obstacles, doing beautiful parallel turns in a majestic display of balance and poise. Such maturity allows us to go up to the high places in the mountains - both physically and spiritually - not just to witness the beauty and grandeur displayed there, but to experience the excitement, satisfaction and fulfilment of being able to journey elegantly and safely through those places, in spite of them being potentially hostile and dangerous. (Psalm 23 v 4).

Christian Parallels | PART 2

Becoming a Different Kind of Animal

One amazing similarity between Skiing and Christianity is that you can only begin to really develop and grow towards maturity if you choose to see yourself transformed into a completely different being. It is only when you do this that whole new areas of opportunity and adventure will open up for you but, if you are unable to do this, you will remain as someone who constantly uses unnecessary amounts of energy without making much progress and be likely to repeatedly fall.

From the age of 8 years I developed a keen interest in camping and in my teens I became actively involved in walking, climbing and lightweight camping. My time growing up through The Boys' Brigade gave me lots of opportunity to be involved in backpacking expeditions and a group of us would use every school holiday and half term break to hitch-hike to some remote part of the UK in order to explore and enjoy these activities. In the early days we learned to build open fires for cooking, regardless of the weather, but later we became much more sophisticated and began using tiny petrol stoves which were much quicker, more efficient and weren't affected by the rain. One of our favourite destinations was the Lake District, in Cumbria. We would invariably travel in twos and agree to meet at a specific map reference before setting off to walk, climb and camp around as much of that area as we possibly could in the time available.

WE MUST REMAIN POSITIVE

On one of these expeditions to the Langdale area, six of us had been walking all day in torrential rain and, in spite of our waterproofs, we were completely soaked through to the skin. We were taking a footpath which led us alongside a field with what looked like a cricket pavilion at the far end. One of us noticed that the door to this hut was being blown back and forth dangerously in the wind. By this time it was quite late in the day so we saw this as God's clear provision to enable us to dry out and cook a meal in comparative comfort. We immediately made the hut our home by hanging up all our wet things and getting the stoves fired up to cook ourselves a meal and dry out our clothes. That night one of our number read from the book of Job:

> *"He draws up the drops of water which distil as rain to the streams, The clouds pour down their moisture and abundant showers fall on mankind.*
>
> *Who can understand how He spreads out the clouds And how He thunders from His pavilion !!!"*

(Job 36 v 27 – 29).

We knew we were in the right place. It is quite amazing just how warm and homely a steam-filled cricket pavilion can become, so, weary and tired, we rolled out our sleeping bags and bedded down for the night. We woke late the next morning, feeling the warmth of the sun on our faces as it streamed through the windows giving us a sense of relaxed contentment as we gazed at the now perfectly clear blue sky. But then, imagine our horror when one of us suddenly yelled out "People !". We quickly scrambled to peer through the lines of clothes and could see men in white, walking towards us throwing a ball to each other. The truth suddenly crashed in on us – it wasn't an angelic visitation, there was to be a cricket match, and we were occupying their pavilion ! Never had any of us dressed and packed so quickly but, as the teams arrived, we left with a smile explaining how we had taken care of their hut throughout the vicious storm.

WE MUST UNDERSTAND BALANCE

It was on one of these trips to The Lake District that I remember indulging in the dangerous activity of scree-running. We had scaled the heights of

Great Gable and, after spending time drinking-in the fantastic views, were beginning our descent when we came across some massive screes cascading down into the valley. A scree is a steep slope made up of billions of rock fragments. Instinctively we launched ourselves onto one of these and rode it with yells and screams of excitement. The mountaineering term for this would be 'glissading', however, the principle here is to remain very upright as you leap from one foot to the other, digging in your heels as firmly as possible. At each stride the stones begin to flow down the hillside so, keeping your dynamic balance you slide with the moving stones. This is actually a dangerous activity and is not to be recommended, apart from which it is not environmentally friendly. In hindsight we were foolish, but the technique required here illustrates a key point about the innate ability we all have when confronted by steep slopes. We naturally choose to lean back and dig in our heels to try to remain stable and try to stop our descent whereas to run the scree it is necessary to keep our weight evenly on each foot as it slides.

We have an innate tendency to adopt the same technique on any slope where we feel there is a potential to slip or lose control. Fuelled by a fear of falling forwards, we tend to lean back towards the slope and put out our hands behind us in anticipation of cushioning any fall. A good example of this would be attempting to walk down a steep grassy embankment. We automatically find ourselves either digging in our heels or twisting round as we lean back to lessen the distance between us and the ground. These responses are hard-wired into our psyche from an early age and become part of the self protection measures we can instantly call upon without any conscious thought or effort. We could use these principles countless times in everyday situations so that they become quite automatic and generally we will have no idea they are being used. Even in our imagination we can conjure the same reactions; for example; try to picture yourself descending a very steep stairway with no handrail, then begin to sense the reactions and physical responses in your mind.

LIMITATIONS AND FREEDOMS

The very first challenge a person faces in learning to ski is to recognise that once they have put on their ski boots and skis they are no longer a traditional human being but have become a completely different animal with quite different advantages and disadvantages. This is where we begin to consider some of the similarities and differences between the developing skier and the new Christian. Once we have taken the first steps in skiing by putting on the gear, a complete change in our thinking becomes necessary. Our old habits and responses become totally ineffective and inappropriate and we now need to develop new ways of responding (2 Corinthians 5 v 17). We have become a totally different kind of being (Ephesians 4 v 22 – 23) and our old nature needs to be refined. One of the old choruses I used to sing as a young Christian seems to sum this up perfectly:

> Let the beauty of Jesus be seen in me,
> All His wondrous compassion and purity.
> O now, Spirit divine,
> All my nature refine,
> 'Til the beauty of Jesus is seen in me.

(Composed by Albert W. T. Orsborn and Tom M. Jones)

Initially this may be quite a frightening concept, because letting go of old established, tried and tested responses is, for anyone, a scary thing to do, but failure to do this will result in massive levels of frustration and an inability to make any real progress. Therefore, in order to develop as a skier, it will involve developing a completely new mindset and it will require a very different mix of skills to be able to control speed and change direction (Romans 12 v 2). With boots and skis on, people no longer have feet, but long planks which make it impossible to walk normally, they can only slide. In addition to this, by far the most difficult thing to grasp here is that leaning back to try to put weight on your heels will always result in disaster. It's the speedboat principle – the front comes up, the speed rapidly increases and any form of control usually disappears completely. On occasions I have witnessed some female novice skiers, who have gone off into the trees mid lesson to relieve themselves without taking off their skis. They have been known to suddenly re-appear flat on their backs screaming down the slope with their salopettes still round their ankles – not a pretty sight. The real battle here takes place in the mind. We must begin to disregard the old patterns of thinking and reasoning, in order to make a conscious choice to take on a completely new mindset (Romans 6 v 7 – 14). We have become different beings now.

A CHANGED MINDSET

When I am wearing my ski gear, my feet are positioned so that my toes are roughly at the centre of each ski and my ski boots are held in the correct

The basic ski posture requires us to adopt a completely different body shape.

position by the ski bindings. This means that my skis protrude some distance both in front of me and behind me which makes the whole idea of digging in my heels a physical impossibility. Furthermore, I now need to understand that the area of my skis which will provide me with the control over my speed and direction is *the front part of my skis* !!! Maintaining some pressure on the front part of the skis therefore becomes an essential requirement for all skiers, yet this is a completely foreign concept to the natural human brain. When I'm on any steep gradient, especially a slippery one, my years of subconscious training and experience have conditioned me to want to lean back onto my heels. To be a skier, however, I have to begin to think and respond to gradients differently and not in the way my natural human brain tells me. If, for whatever reason, I am unable or unwilling to do this, I will never become an accomplished skier.

STANDING AS A CHRISTIAN

Exactly the same principle (though it's nothing to do with gradients), applies to people who want to live their lives in accordance with the principles of the Christian faith. Once we have made the decision to become a Christian and surrendered our lives to Jesus as our Saviour and Lord, it is so important that we begin to think and respond differently to our everyday surroundings and not just try to carry on as we have done previously (Galatians 4 v 9). If, for whatever reason, we are unable or unwilling to do this, our lives will be a constant battle for survival and we will repeatedly fall. The basic principle here, whether attempting to grow as a skier or a Christian, is that a completely different attitude of mind is required. Furthermore, whatever people tell you, it will only work for you if you actually discover how to do it for yourself. No wonder Paul needed to write so emphatically:

> *"I tell you this, and insist on it in The Lord, that you must no longer live as the Gentiles do – in the futility of their thinking" (Ephesians 4 v 17).*

We must begin to realise that our pre-Christian patterns of thinking and responding are simply no longer appropriate for us if we want to thrive in our new role as children of God. The real exhilaration and freedom of the Christian life comes from choosing to follow the example and the teachings of Jesus. Our old practices, many of which have become deeply ingrained through years of constant repetition, must now be surrendered, released and replaced with the solid teaching of the Scriptures.

All through the New Testament the message is constantly repeated for us to repent, turn, and be different. People often get confused about the difference between confession and repentance and then, after confessing their sins to God, cannot understand why they still seem to be weighed down with the same burdens. On a Tuesday, where I live, the local authority refuse disposal wagon comes down my street. If I open my front door and shout to the men "I want you to know that I've got piles of rubbish in my house !". That is confession – but I've still got the rubbish. Instead, I need to put it all into a plastic bag, run down the path and give it to the men and say "Here's my rubbish, please take it away, I never want to see it again" - that's repentance. Repentance actually means making a 180 degree change of direction – a complete turnaround – and this must begin in our minds. That's the reason many people fail to keep their New Year resolutions – no real change has taken place in their mind. Our minds, what we think and what we repeatedly tell ourselves, are the key here. Paul put it like this: -

> "Do not conform any longer to the pattern of this world, but be transformed by the renewing of your mind. Then you will be able to prove for yourselves what is the good, acceptable and perfect will of God" (Romans 12 v 2).

A DIFFICULT CHOICE

Like most things, the acid test here is, 'can this really be proved or is it just a theory?' Many people will say that it is impossible to actually prove the existence of God, but this is a lie. It is definitely possible to prove the existence of God with 100% certainty. The difficulty here is that you cannot prove it to anyone else and nobody else can prove it to you. It can only be proved when someone wants to experience a personal relationship with Jesus Christ. You can only know for certain that the front part of your skis will enable you to control your speed and direction, once you have experienced it for yourself. As long as you continue to lean back and allow your past experiences to dictate how you behave, you will continue to struggle, and fall (2 Peter 1 v 10).

As believers, Paul reminds us that because of what Jesus has done for us on the cross, we are no longer slaves to our old nature. Therefore we have no need to allow our past experiences to dictate how we should respond. It is important here to recognise the difference between helpful lessons we have learned and may want to keep, as opposed to any unhelpful patterns we have developed and need to change. People will often try to justify their behaviour by reasoning "Well, I can't help it, that's just the way I am". My usual reply to this is: "Well that may well have been the case for you in the past, but you actually have the choice now about whether you want to stay like that or not" (Joshua 24 v 15).

LEARNING HOW TO EXERCISE CONTROL

A Christian lady came to me for help many years ago about her foul temper because her family were exasperated by her apparent complete inability to exercise any control over it. She had asked God to help her and been prayed for on numerous occasions but it had made no difference. She could lose her temper in a fraction of a second and erupt like a volcano. A few seconds later it would all be over for her, but her family would be left cowering in corners and afraid to say anything. She said to me "Well, I can't help it, it's just the way I am". Her outbursts were feared by the people with whom she worked and even her close friends often felt they were 'walking on eggshells'. She told me that she had been like this for most of her life and that she was completely unable to control these powerful outbursts but just had to let them happen. We had been working together on this for a few weeks, during which time she told me repeatedly that she had no control over this, until one day she spoke about a specific incident that had happened a few days earlier. As she was leaving work that day, her boss caught up with her in the car park and said something to her which really annoyed her. She leaped into her car, drove home at a violent speed (a distance of about 3 miles), rushed into her house, slammed the door and exploded to her husband who was innocently cooking their tea. When I explained how excited I was about this, she looked at me with blank disbelief. I said, "You have just demonstrated to me that you are perfectly capable of controlling your emotional outbursts because you held this one for over 20 minutes while you drove home and then chose to 'lose it' where you felt it would have the biggest impact! Now you must learn how to exercise this control on every other occasion". She genuinely didn't think this was possible for her, but now could no longer deny what she had experienced. She was now able to begin work on how to develop her 'new-found' ability.

A NEW CREATION

The good ski instructor will be constantly trying to encourage his pupils to switch off what their human brain is automatically telling them and switch onto their new 'ski brain'. This will involve them making the choice to press forward in their boots and down on their toes, which will transfer pressure onto the front of their skis, and to learn to feel that this is actually enabling them to control their direction and speed. To the novice, this can be scary and painful, and many people simply can't bring themselves to believe that it will work, so continue to struggle and fall. In the Christian life we are urged to put away what our past experiences in the world are telling us and move into new levels of faith and trust as followers of Jesus. This becomes an on-going internal struggle, to break out of our old ways of thinking and begin to apply the dynamic principles of The Bible. Paul described it like this:-

"For in my inner being I delight in God's law, but I see another law at work in the members of my body, waging war against the law of my mind and making me a prisoner of the law of sin at work within my members".

(Romans 7 v 22-23)

A DIFFERENT MINDSET

As long as we continue to be controlled by our old ways of thinking we will be unable to move into the new levels of freedom that await us and sometimes it will just seem impossible to make this shift. Paul talks, in Romans 7 v 15-20, about the frustration of wanting to be different yet ending up falling into the same patterns of behaviour as in the past. So, what is the secret? It is to stop beating ourselves up about this and learn to trust that God has designed us to be made and equipped as a completely different kind of being.

"Therefore, if anyone is in Christ he is a new creation; the old has gone and the new has come" (2 Corinthians 5 v 17)

... "with regard to your former way of life, to put off your old self which is being corrupted by its deceitful desires; to be made new in the attitude of your minds; and to put on the new self..." (Ephesians 4 v 22-24)

We will never be able to grow into maturity until we begin to grasp the amazing reality that we are not anymore the same person we have been in the past. Therefore we need to be open to learn new ways of doing things and not simply carry on doing what once worked for us. Somebody's definition of a miracle is: 'Continuing to do what you've always done but expecting a different outcome'. Someone else said, "If you always do what you've always done, you will always get what you've always got!".

NEW HORIZONS

One of the most debilitating aspects of becoming a new being in Christ is that we keep going back to focus on all the things we think we're not allowed to do anymore. That mentality will keep us firmly rooted in the past with continual feelings of regret and disappointment and an increasing desire to want to return to those experiences. Instead, we must begin to look ahead to the amazing opportunities and adventures God holds out for us if we will simply trust Him and be obedient to Him. This commences with us receiving a new understanding of who we have now become, 'in Him' (Romans 8 v 1 – 2).

Paul often addresses his letters to 'the saints', meaning the sanctified ones, and explains that God does not treat us as foreigners or aliens but as members of the precious family He has specifically chosen. I become a saint in God's sight once I have accepted that Jesus died to pay the penalty for my sin, that I am therefore forgiven and cleansed by His unique sacrifice and so I choose to invite Him into my life as my Saviour and Lord. Saviour means that He has saved me from the judgement God will one day mete out against all the sinful, evil things of this world, and Lord means that I choose to surrender everything I am, everything I possess, and everything I desire, to be directed and governed by Him for the rest of my life (2 Peter 1 v 11). This is the beginning of real spiritual development and gives me the potential to grow towards spiritual maturity.

WHAT IF I CAN'T DO IT ?

The Bible tells me that, even before I was aware of it, God had already put in place everything I would need and I simply have to accept and receive what he has done for me to be able to live and move in this new dimension (Ephesians 1 v 3 – 4). I can never earn or deserve these privileges, they are a free gift from the heart of a loving heavenly Father. God has a specific plan and destiny for me and this can be hard to believe, so it is only as I choose to step out in faith and be obedient to Him, that I will be able to prove for myself the reality of His Word.

Jesus enters my life, at my invitation, in the form of the Holy Spirit and He begins to effect changes in me from the inside. As I open myself to receive more of Him, His beautiful qualities begin to be seen in me. As I choose to confess my weaknesses and failures by submitting my old nature to Him, the fruits (qualities) of His Holy Spirit: Love, Joy, Peace, Faithfulness, Gentleness, Kindness, Goodness, Patience and Self Control (Galatians 5 v 22) begin to make an impact on my choices and decisions. I begin to see things differently and start to view myself, other people and the whole world from His perspective instead of from my own blinkered and distorted standpoint. I begin to believe that I am indeed seated with Christ in the heavenly realms (Ephesians 2 v 6) and that He has an amazing plan and purpose for my life. I can learn to genuinely rejoice in every situation and begin to see every obstacle as an opportunity, and begin to turn every negative attitude into a positive one, and begin to experience victory and success instead of defeat and depression. I am now in a position to begin to see how God has made it possible for me to actually become a completely different person (1 Samuel 10 v 6).

Christian Parallels | PART 3

Choosing the Right Equipment

E very sport or activity of any sort is made so much more difficult when you don't have the right equipment available. Imagine trying to decorate a room without having the most appropriate brushes, ladders and rollers, or trying to do maintenance work on a car engine without having the correct spanners or tools. Everything is likely to become more complicated, sometimes even dangerous, and we can quickly lose any sense of enjoyment from doing things when we don't have the right equipment for the job. Understanding this principle is absolutely vital when we talk about skiing and it is equally significant in terms of living out the Christian life. It is not just a question of being successful at what we do, but about being able to become more proficient whilst experiencing a genuine sense of fun and enjoyment at the same time. It is also not simply about adhering to a set of rules or regulations, although there are important principles to be borne in mind here. It is about growing and developing by having confidence that our equipment is designed to help us perform efficiently, safely and to the best of our ability.

The incredible thing about living the Christian life is that God has already provided everything we need to be powerful and effective, even before we knew that we had the need, and He has fashioned each element to be a perfect fit for each one of us (2 Peter 1 v 3 - 10). Every aspect of the Christian's spiritual equipment has been lovingly prepared by God and is made freely available to us. All we need to do is recognise these tools, receive them, make them our own and begin to use them for His glory. Then our lives will take on a whole new dimension and, with inexplicable levels of excitement, we will find ourselves journeying more quickly towards spiritual maturity.

SKI BOOTS

The first item of ski equipment we are going to consider here is the choice of a pair of ski boots. Ski boots look and feel heavy, awkward and ungainly and it is difficult to imagine how anyone could do anything once they have put them on. They are constructed with a tough, rigid exterior that is designed to resist very high impacts, they have a softer inner boot which is intended to be comfortable and warm. They are designed to come high up your leg to give vital protection to your ankle joint, and the whole boot is angled so as to push your lower leg forward into a flexed position which makes the task of standing upright extremely difficult. The boots are hinged to allow a slight amount of forward movement but their rigidity prevents any sideways movement that would put unnecessary pressure on your ankle joint. Your boots must be a really snug fit allowing no movement of your foot inside the boot, thereby making sure that every little movement is actually transmitted down onto the ski. Extra padding is often needed around the ankles and shins to relieve pressure on the bones and to ensure a snug fit without cutting off the blood supply. It usually takes people a while to get used to having their feet clamped in this way and whilst we tend to think that eventually the boots will mould to the shape of our feet, it actually feels as though our feet get moulded into the shape of the boots. However, we are not going to be able to function effectively unless we get reasonably comfortable in our ski boots. I skied for nearly 10 years in a pair of top quality Nordica boots that I had modified with lots of extra internal padding so that they were an exceptionally good fit for me. Because of this, I was happy to wear them all day every day without feeling any discomfort at all.

RESTRICTIVE OR PROTECTIVE ?

For the novice skier, it will sometimes seem totally unnecessary, highly restrictive, and often quite painful to have your feet held so securely in this way, yet it is this very security that will provide the protection you need and that will facilitate your ability to ski successfully. Understanding our relationship with God can appear to some people as similarly restrictive and sometimes equally painful. He can sometimes appear to be hard and rigid like the outer shell of the ski boot, holding us tightly and restricting our movement. The Bible tells us that His desire is to hold us securely so that we are protected from the harmful pressures of this life. Furthermore, He wants to restrict us from any movement that would be counter-productive or stop us from growing and becoming strong in Him. He does this to help us function to the very best of our ability in the way we were designed because He knows that we can only experience real satisfaction and fulfilment when we choose to live by His standards (Psalm 139 v 7 - 10).

When we consider the inner ski boot, we can see a very different side of God's nature. This is soft and well padded and reminds us of the way Jesus comes into our lives and envelops us with the warmth and softness of His beautiful qualities. When we begin the Christian life we generally have little idea what kind of pressures or problems we are going to encounter so it gives us great encouragement to know that God will never leave us or forsake us, that He holds us firmly in the palm of His hand (Isaiah 49 v 15-16) and that He covers us with His protection every day of our lives. However, many people can misunderstand God acting this way on our behalf and believe He is too controlling. Some people believe the Christian life is dominated by a set of outdated rules aimed at stopping us from doing all the things we enjoy the most. They don't seem to understand that to actually live as a Christian we need to become a completely different kind of being and, as such, will be unable to operate without adopting some completely new principles. If we are to face the real world and endure the hardships that come as a result of this, we need to know that we are being held firmly so that absolutely nothing will be able to destroy the plans and purposes God has for our lives.

OUR SKIS MUST BE SOLID YET FLEXIBLE

The next item of equipment for us to consider is the choice of a pair of skis. When I started skiing, the right length of ski for a person was judged to be up to 40cms above their head height. In those days, the construction of skis was not as sophisticated as it is now, so it was deemed necessary to have skis of that length in order to adequately support the person's weight over the whole length of the ski. This made the skis much more difficult to control, and therefore learning to ski was a much slower process. My first skis, made by Atomic, were 205cms long even though I was only 183cms tall, however years later I settled for a pair of Dynastar Geant 185's on which I skied very happily for many years. Nowadays getting the right ski for someone is more to do with its construction than with its length alone. Modern skis are made up of a mixture of many different components including plastics, metals, and carbon-fibre. These prevent the ski from flexing or twisting inappropriately and enable them to withstand the massive pressures that can be encountered during a ski run. The technical construction makes it possible for the skis to flex at certain points yet hold their shape when the skier is making turns. They require a combination of immense strength along with appropriate flexibility to be able to perform effectively. Therefore, when you come to choose a ski, the technician is likely to talk to you about your standard of ski experience and your weight before advising you about the flex patterns of skis that would be most appropriate for you. Getting a ski that is right for you will make all the difference in the world to your levels of enjoyment, fulfilment and achievement as a skier. It therefore also needs to be said that any sense of satisfaction and progress in skiing will quickly disappear if you end up with an inappropriate pair of skis.

Just like our skis, we need to know that we are standing on a strong, smooth base which is lubricated with the wax of faithful prayer, relevant for the circumstances of the moment. This allows us to move forward gracefully and not stick to the world under our feet. We need to know that we have the security of being kept on track by the sharp metal edges of sound, consistent Bible teaching which will help prevent us from slipping or skidding off course. The solid platforms we develop within the church to which we belong should be those that will support us with strength and stability as we face the trials and tribulations of living in a secular world. Yet there must also be sufficient flexibility in the structure of the organisation to allow us to ride the bumps and hollows of life without being thrown off balance.

SKI BINDINGS MUST HOLD US SECURELY YET BE ABLE TO RELEASE US WHEN NECESSARY

In addition to making the right choice of ski, you also need to consider which bindings will be most suitable for you. Ski bindings are those highly engineered and sophisticated pieces of equipment that are fixed to the ski in order to hold your ski boots in place. They have the dual job of holding each boot firmly so that it doesn't move about on the ski, yet are able to release your boot from the ski in the event of a twist or a fall. There are some variations here, but generally, in the event of a fall, the toe pieces are designed to release the boot in a sideways direction whereas the heel pieces are designed to release the boot in an upward and forward direction. It is absolutely vital that the bindings are fitted and adjusted correctly by someone who is trained and qualified to do this. Each boot must be held quite securely so that every tiny movement of the foot can be transmitted directly onto the ski. Bindings that are not fitted and adjusted correctly will create dangerous problems for the skier by either releasing the boot from the ski too easily or not releasing the boot easily enough. Either of these could result in painful stresses being inflicted onto the knee and ankle joints which could easily cause serious injuries.

Just like the ski bindings, we need to have confidence that we are being held firmly within a body of believers (a church), so that our actions and responses can be used positively at every opportunity. We must have confidence that, although we are being held firmly, we can be released spiritually whenever the occasion demands it (Romans 12 v 4 - 8). Ski bindings ensure that we are standing in the right place to be able to use our skills effectively and we need the same sense of security from our church family. God has already equipped us with skills talents and abilities but it is our responsibility to continue to develop these and to use them for the expansion of His kingdom. This is the only way we can keep moving towards spiritual maturity (1 Peter 4 v 10).

SKI POLES

The only other item of ski hardware for us to consider is the ski poles and I liken these to our Christian friends. We may be able to cope from time to time without them, but they are designed to be a great encouragement and support to us (Exodus 17 v 11 - 13). Ski poles can help to push us along when we are moving on the flat, they can provide support and balance when we are climbing up a gradient, they can help to hold us steady when we are stepping round on a slippery slope, and they can be an aide to good balance when we are skiing down the hill. As we continue to develop, learning how to use the ski poles correctly will help keep our upper body in the right position and make us better prepared each time we want to initiate a ski turn. However, just like the other items of equipment, it is important to get ones that are right for us. In the event that the poles are either too long or too short, our skiing ability will be hampered, they will become a liability and it would be a matter of some urgency to replace them as soon as possible (2 Timothy 3 v 1 - 5). Therefore, we should choose our friends carefully because we want them to be an asset, not a hindrance.

We may be able to get by in life for a time without friends, but they can be great source of support when times are hard. We want them to push us along when we are spiritually flat, we want their assistance when we are climbing to new heights, we want their support when we are turning towards something new, we want them to help keep us balanced when we are flying smoothly along and we want their expertise in initiating refinements and adjustments that will help to control our speed and direction in the Christian life. Friends that are too powerful or too weak will be of little help to us in times of difficulty so we need to cultivate a good relationship with people we can rely upon and who are themselves spiritually mature.

Christian Parallels | PART 4

Wearing the Right Clothing

It appeared, in the early days, that skiing was only for the rich and famous because everything seemed so expensive, but in more recent times everything to do with ski clothing seems to have become intertwined with the fashion industry. It seems right therefore to ask:- "Should the emphasis be upon Function or Fashion" ? My answer is quite straight forward, when it comes to suitable clothing, our main concern must always be 'function'. However, it is perfectly OK to wear functional garments that are fashionable too, but it is definitely not OK to wear fashionable garments that are not functional.

Over the years, there have been too many serious accidents in the mountains which have been caused by people wearing inappropriate clothing. We must be careful not to have too casual a view about enjoying the mountain environment without showing it the proper respect. We should not hold onto a 'picture-postcard' image of clear blue skies, beautiful soft snow and brilliant sunshine without also remembering that the skiing environment is potentially a very dangerous one. To be inadequately or inappropriately dressed is to be complacent and court danger. It could wreck our own enjoyment as well as put other people's lives at risk.

UNDERGARMENTS

We must never forget that, by very nature, skiing happens on snow, which is frozen water, often at high altitudes and in mountainous environments where the weather can be quite hostile at times. There can also be, depending on your level of skiing ability, the occasional long periods of inactivity such as waiting in lift queues, sitting on chair lifts or standing in line before a ski instructor. Even short periods of inactivity can have a chilling effect on the body in this climate, so the value of wearing some good quality insulation undergarments should be seen as essential. Thermal vests and long-johns therefore really are a necessity to keep up your core body temperature. If this should begin to fall, it is vital to retreat immediately to somewhere warm and safe to recuperate.

Undergarments remind me it is not what other people can see of me on the outside that is really important, but what is going on for me internally that I have to be most concerned about. I must continually be aware of my internal spiritual temperature and if, for any reason, this begins to drop I should take immediate action to remedy the situation. This is about being attentive to my personal relationship with God and whether I am being adversely affected by issues that are happening around me. In all the excitement and activity of my environment, it is easy to overlook the foundational aspects of my faith, so I must regularly give myself a quick reality check. The following seven basic elements (covered in more detail in our Gateway to Life booklet 'Moving Forward') that are required to sustain any form of life on earth, is a useful starting point:

a) am I talking to, and hearing from, God every day? (Air),

b) am I living every day with the light of Jesus in my life as Saviour and Lord? (Light),

c) am I absorbing nourishment from The Bible every day? (Food),

d) am I daily surrendering to the supernatural power of The Holy Spirit? (Water),

e) am I receiving encouragement every day from the people of God? (Warmth),

f) am I confessing and turning from my sin every day? (Excretion),

g) am I demonstrating and sharing my faith with others every day? (Reproduction).

ONLY POSSESSING THEM OR ACTUALLY WEARING THEM?

Even when I know that all these foundation garments are in my possession, I must still check whether I'm actually wearing them ! To be certain of this I now ask myself some further searching questions to see if there's any evidence, such as:

i.   am I beginning to be negative or critical?
ii.   have I lost my objectivity in any way?
iii. do I find it hard to genuinely praise God?
iv.   am I constantly annoyed or frustrated?
v.   am I getting more impatient with others?
vi.   am I withdrawing in some way or becoming more inward looking?
vii. have I stopped using my gifts to help others?
viii. do I find myself regularly making a big issue out of trivial things?
ix.   am I struggling with the time I spend reading The Bible and talking to God?
x.   am I getting over-tired doing routine things?
xi.   do I make everything all about me?
xii. are small and comparatively insignificant things upsetting me?
xiii. do I get bothered by the standards of other people's ministry?
xiv. am I increasingly comparing myself to others?
xv.   am I convinced that I can cope on my own?

Whatever answers I come up with to questions like this will give me some clear warning signs about whether or not my spiritual temperature is taking a dive and it could be really helpful for me to give myself a spiritual health check like this from time to time. Out on the snow, whenever I feel that I am starting to grow cold I must immediately increase my activity levels and urgently get myself into an environment where I can begin to warm up again. From a spiritual point of view, if I detect such a change happening to me it can be quite beneficial to discuss this with a trusted friend or a mature Christian, but failure to take any action in this regard would be an indication of great immaturity. In a spiritual sense, I need to be built up by being both challenged and encouraged by the warmth of good fellowship. It is not uncommon, when undertaking an exercise like this, for other issues to begin to surface so it can also be beneficial to speak to a qualified Christian counsellor who will be able to help me identify and deal with any underlying issues. If my undergarments are scrunched up in any way, I am going to be very uncomfortable and they won't be able to do their job properly. It is important, therefore, for me to get any underlying issues straightened out however nice my outward appearance might appear to be. I really must pay careful attention to my spiritual core temperature if I am to prevent my journey towards spiritual maturity from being shipwrecked.

3. Every part of ski clothing is designed to provide protection against the severe weather that can be encountered in the mountains

OUTER GARMENTS

The main outer garments worn by skiers will generally fall into the following categories; a one-piece ski suit, or a ski jacket, with either ski pants or salopettes. These will usually be made of a fairly tough, moisture proof outer fabric with a high quality synthetic insulation material in the lining. They need to be windproof and weatherproof to quite a high degree and have high heat retention qualities to cope with the serious weather conditions that can often be encountered in the mountains. These garments are frequently made in bright, fashionable colours and styles for high visibility and may often contain an emergency tracking device. Because the clothing is so distinctive, it is quite common to begin to recognise people by what they wear on the ski slopes and then not to recognise them when they are in more casual dress at other times.

The outer garments of the skier draw my attention to the main areas of gifting and ministry with which God has endowed us. I believe that God has given to every person (there are no exceptions here) a specific mixture of gifts, skills, talents and abilities that He wants us to use for the establishing and extending of His kingdom here on earth. It is only as we choose to put on these qualities and wear them appropriately that we will discover the amazing blessings He has in store for us. It would be foolish for us to venture out into the mountains dressed in the clothing we have grown accustomed to wearing at work, or around the house. So we must not underestimate the importance of putting on those things God has provided for us and not believe that we can simply carry on in the Christian life without this provision. Similarly, we must not fall into the trap of trying to be trendy and fashionable at the expense of being true to the principles of God's Word. As we venture into the outside world God does not want us to be poorly equipped or inadequately dressed but has prepared the very finest things for us. He demonstrates this in, what I think is, one of the most incredible passages in the whole Bible. As you read this, allow every word to impact your soul:

> *"God's divine power has given us everything we need for life and godliness through our knowledge of Him who called us by His own glory and goodness. Through these He has given us His very great and precious promises so that through them you may participate in the divine nature*

and escape the corruption in the world caused by evil desires. For this very reason, make every effort to add to your faith goodness; and to goodness, knowledge; and to knowledge, self control; and to self control, perseverance; and to perseverance, godliness; and to godliness, brotherly kindness; and to brotherly kindness, love. For if you possess these qualities in increasing measure they will keep you from being ineffective and unproductive in your knowledge of our Lord Jesus Christ. But if anyone does not have them, he is short sighted and blind and has forgotten that he has been cleansed from his past sins. Therefore, my brothers, be all the more eager to make your calling and election sure. For if you do these things you will never fall and you will receive a rich welcome into the eternal kingdom of our Lord and Saviour Jesus Christ".

(2 Peter 2 v 3 - 11)

How utterly amazing is that ? God furnishes us with exactly what we need to be able to participate with Him in the work He has called us to do. (Every skier should underline the words; "For if you do these things you will never fall !") Whilst God has provided everything for us, we can see here that we are still required to exercise our human responsibility too. Someone once said

"Our responsibility is our response to His ability"

FIRSTLY, THE ARMOUR

Now let us consider what God's spiritual clothing looks like as we review what the apostle Paul says to the Ephesians; "Put on the full armour of God so that you will be able to stand" ! (Ephesians 6 v 10). This is all about continuing to be able to stand in the hostile environment of the world. We need to be sure that every piece is securely in place so it can provide the protection that will enable us to continue to stand against the attacks of the enemy. One of the most overlooked pieces of this armour is the Belt of Truth without which all the other parts become useless. Truth always begins with ourselves, so learning to be brutally honest with ourselves first is a key requirement for our journey towards maturity. One of the biggest stumbling blocks in the life of the Christian church today, is the inability of people to be honest with one another. For some inexplicable reason many people grow up with the thinking that it is unchristian for us to disagree and so end up being untruthful. We must cultivate the habit of being honest instead of simply trying to keep up appearances.

Next, Paul draws our attention to 'the breastplate of righteousness'. Here we understand the importance of being right with God in all our dealings, knowing that we are cleansed, purified and made holy in His sight by the precious blood of Jesus. We must not underestimate the significance of this if we are to stand at all in the world.

Having our feet fitted with the readiness that comes from the gospel of peace, reminds us that we are required to be constantly prepared and alert for the Kingdom. Being ready to step out in faith is one thing, but we need to remember that, in stepping out, we are required to be messengers of peace. So often the messages we convey can be judgemental and include frustration, anger, disappointment or criticism.

The shield of faith is such a powerful piece of armour. The Bible reminds us that God has given every person a portion of faith (Romans 12 v 3, Ephesians 2 v 8) but, like a muscle, this only grows to become strong as we exercise it. Failure to use it will result in it weakening and becoming insignificant to the point where we will be uncertain of it.

Protecting the head is always necessary, for obvious reasons, so we need the certainty and confidence that comes from having the helmet of salvation firmly in place. We are physically and spiritually unable to stand whenever our head is in a spin. Nothing in the world will make any real sense to us until we know that our salvation in Jesus is absolutely secure.

The sword of The Spirit is given to us primarily for our defence and to enable us to stand, so we must be diligent in learning how to use it. It is The Word of God and it is sharper than a two-edged sword, so handling it effectively takes strength, courage and skill. Any weapon is most dangerous when in the hands of an unskilled person, but most effective in the hands of someone trained in its application.

The final piece of armour described here is 'praying in the Spirit'. All the other pieces of armour will prove to be ineffective defences against the attacks of the enemy unless they are knit together in an attitude of faithful, believing prayer. We are instructed to use this on all occasions and in all kinds of ways

Some people may say that you should remember to put on the armour of God first thing every morning, whereas others will tell you that you should never take it off. Whatever your views may be about this, one thing is certain, the armour of God is very necessary to protect us as we seek to make a stand, and continue to stand, in the outside world.

SECONDLY, THE POWER

When Jesus talked to his disciples about the time when He would send them The Holy Spirit, He said "Stay in the city until you have been clothed with power from on high" (Luke 24 v 49). One of the distinct ministries of the Holy Spirit is to 'clothe' us with His power. That means He will come upon us, cover us, drench us, or saturate us with His qualities. These qualities are the supernatural gifts of Wisdom, Knowledge, Faith, Healings, Miracles, Prophecy, Discernment, Tongues and the Interpretation of Tongues (1 Corinthians 12 v 8 – 11). They are all freely given by the same Holy Spirit who came into our lives at our invitation when we were saved, and are therefore available to every believer – no exceptions. How amazing that God chooses to clothe us in these supernatural qualities that will make us stand out like bright lights in the darkness of the world. Like the skier's outer garments, we must choose to put them on and wear them correctly to show that we are grateful for His provision and are proud to belong to such a loving, gracious, heavenly Father. However, unlike the outer garments of the skier, these qualities are given to us primarily so that we can minister God's grace to the benefit of other people.

THIRDLY, THE ROLES

Our spiritual outer garments also include some specific roles that Jesus has given to us. Paul writes, "But to each one of us grace has been given as Christ apportioned it" (Ephesians 4 v 7). He then goes on to identify 5 key areas of ministry which are given for building up other people in their journey towards maturity. These are:

Apostles – these are the pioneers of the kingdom, those who develop plans and create structure, they are visionary planters and builders, breaking new ground.

Prophets – these are the people who hear God and speak out His Word, clearly and boldly, both in foretelling and forth-telling.

Evangelists – these are the preachers who can present the gospel in attractive ways that hold people's attention and draw them into the kingdom.

Pastors – these are the shepherds who demonstrate real care and concern for people's welfare and guide them into the 'green pastures' of truth.

Teachers – these are the people who are able to explain the truths of the Bible in logical, constructive ways that others can appreciate and understand.

We all possess some elements of each of these qualities but we will generally be drawn to one particular role depending on the circumstances we are in at the time. Although not everyone may feel that they have one of these 'ministries', we are all capable of pioneering something for the kingdom or of explaining the gospel to someone who is interested. We are all capable of boldly speaking the Word of God into a person's life, or caring for someone who is in need. Just like the outer garments of the skier, we are able to put on whatever is most appropriate for that situation that day. These are spiritual garments that God has provided and, like other key kingdom qualities, as we choose to use them for the benefit of others, we continue to grow towards maturity.

JUMPERS AND GILETS

Apart from shirts or blouses, as skiers, we may sometimes feel the need for additional layers of insulation between our undergarments and our outer garments. These layers will generally be hidden under the outer garments but on occasions, when the conditions are right, they may be worn without the usual outer garments. Some of these may be brightly coloured whereas others may not stand out quite so much. For the Christian, these extra layers include a whole range of spiritual activities such as: encouraging, giving, administering, organising, helping, facilitating, or serving. Once again, we all have the capacity to be involved in each of these ways, depending on the circumstances at the time, and should therefore be willing to exercise these qualities by responding to people's needs as we become aware of them (Romans 12 v 4 – 8). We should not underestimate the importance of these extra layers of ministry because so often they will be the means of allowing others to fulfil their areas of gifting more fully. Nor should we assume that these are only carried out by people who don't have a more prominent gift or ministry. Sometimes this can be used as an excuse by people who wish to stay behind the scenes but this is a false humility and can be a way of avoiding opportunities to develop and grow. It is only as each one of us becomes aware of the responsibility we have, both to one another and to the kingdom of God, that we will be able to function effectively and keep growing towards maturity (Ephesians 4 v 16 and 1 Peter 4 v 10).

HATS, HELMETS AND SCARVES

It is a fact that the majority of heat loss from the body occurs through the head so, when skiing in what is generally a very cold environment, wearing appropriate head and neck covering is a good way of keeping warm. The use of ski helmets has also become a commonly accepted method of good protection as well as warmth, and a scarf fills the gap around the neck to prevent any cold air or snow from reaching us which might lower our core temperature. When Paul writes about the armour of God (Ephesians 6 v 10 - 12), he emphasises that it is all for our protection and reminds us that we need to have the helmet of salvation securely in place. This equates to having the certainty of knowing who we are and whose we are, before we venture into any unfamiliar or dangerous territory. The protection of our head is paramount so that we can keep our minds focused. Paul writes:

"Those who live according to the sinful nature have their minds set on what that nature desires, but those who live in accordance with the Spirit have their minds set on what the Spirit desires" (Romans 8 v 5).

Our spiritual core temperature will tend to drop quickly if our head is not being appropriately and properly protected. We will soon begin to lose the ability to think and reason in line with the Word of God and relapse into our old ways of thinking and behaving. We will forget that we have been adopted into the family of God, that we are now different people, and will resort to the old self-protection measures which are dictated to us by our 'old-nature'. Tensions will start to creep in as we develop increased feelings of stress and oppression. It is so easy for us to go back to what we have done in the past that, generally, we won't even realise that we are doing it.

GOGGLES AND GLASSES

People who enjoy activities in the mountains can experience many different weather conditions, any of which could put strain on the eyes, so good quality eye protection is essential. Because of the altitude, dangerously high levels of ultra violet rays from the sun, as well as reflected glare from the snow, can result in serious damage to the eyes. There also may be times when a stiff wind is cutting across the ground or when tiny particles of snow and ice are whipped up by the wind. There could be times when beautiful snowflakes float gently down from above or tiny ice crystals, each one perfect and unique, fill the air. There may be times of blizzard when the wind drives the snow horizontally, or periods of 'white-out' where it is impossible to distinguish the ground from the sky. In soft snow, or powder, the spray from the front of the skis will sometimes be hitting the skier blindingly full in the face. There will be times when, surrounded by mist or cloud, normal visibility becomes impossible. In all these, as well as other conditions, good quality eye protection becomes vital. Without this, people can quickly become disorientated and can make inappropriate, even foolish, choices and occasionally people may suffer from snow-blindness. This is extremely painful and can result in permanent loss of sight. In situations like this we can recognise that, no matter how hard we try, we simply cannot see as clearly as we'd like and, without good quality eye protection, may eventually not be able to see anything at all.

In the Christian life we must be equally diligent to protect ourselves against receiving into our lives the harmful ways of the world. Jesus said:

> *"The eye is the lamp of the body. If your eyes are good, your whole body will be full of light. But if your eyes are bad, your whole body will be full of darkness"*

> *(Matthew 6 v 22 - 23).*

We are aware that everything we see affects us in one way or another, so the world we are living in will continue to impact the choices and decisions we make on a daily basis. We must learn, therefore, to be extremely careful about what we allow into our lives through our eyes, in fact, literally, what we choose to look at. The Bible tells us that God sees us through the filter of the blood of Jesus. He sees us cleansed and purified from our sins, He sees us as righteous and holy, whole and complete in Him. In a similar way we must begin to look at the world through the blood of Jesus, so that we can see His way opening clearly before us and the distractions and attractions of the world pale into insignificance in comparison. "Let us fix our eyes on Jesus, the author and perfecter of our faith" (Hebrews 12 v 2).

GLOVES AND SOCKS

We come now to consider the last of the items of clothing which the skier will need – those items intended to keep our extremities warm. The choice of socks is one mainly of personal preference since much of the warmth and protection is already provided by the ski boots. However, some people like thick socks for extra comfort whereas others prefer thin socks for a better sense of being held firmly within their boots. Either way, the important factor here is to maintain good circulation at all times. Once the toes get cold and the circulation slows down, the feet become very painful and then exercising control over the skis becomes much more difficult. The choice of ski gloves is a little more straight forward because it is quite obvious that fingers are going to need protection against the cold. Skiers would be well advised to get the best quality gloves they can afford, with the best quality insulation, and maybe even purchase some lightweight inner gloves as well. We can easily overlook the importance of adequately protecting our extremities, yet many people will have had the experience of not being able to function properly when their fingers and toes are frozen. Similarly, you will know, if you have ever hit your finger with a hammer, how any form of sensible communication becomes almost impossible when you are experiencing excruciating pain.

In the Christian life it is equally important for us to protect our extremities and not allow our spiritual temperature to fall. I define our extremities as the areas of our life that are at the very edge of our contact with the non-Christian world. This can include the places where we work or study, our neighbours, friends, clubs or societies, where we socialise and where we live, in fact, wherever we are in contact with people. Protecting these areas of our life means first of all, covering them in prayer by laying everything and every situation before The Lord on a daily basis. A good policy is to pray through each aspect of the day as you see it in the morning, and then give thanks for everything in the evening, regardless of the outcome. Following this principle will help to keep the circulation of the Holy Spirit in these edges of your Christian life and will, in turn, help to maintain your spiritual core temperature. Additional insulation in these areas can be obtained by choosing to make yourself accountable to a mature Christian friend. Having regular discussions and praying together about your witness can make a really positive impact on the way you are able to handle whatever situations, circumstances or people you may be required to face on a daily basis.

Christian Parallels | PART 5

Understanding the Environment

I am very fortunate to have been able to spend so much time in my teens and twenties walking and climbing in the hills and mountains. As an outdoor activity enthusiast, I took every possible opportunity to get away and enjoy the beautiful scenery in locations all around the UK and Europe. On one occasion when a group of us were camping near Interlaken in Switzerland we had spent the whole morning hiking and scrambling to the top of an 800 metre high ridge. We had then walked along the ridge until we reached a point where the whole valley was laid out in front of us. We could see for miles as the valley stretched out into the distance. We sat in the sunshine to eat our packed lunches while identifying tiny villages and hamlets far away on the valley floor. Suddenly, one of us turned to look behind and saw black clouds sweeping along the valley towards us. A thunder storm was approaching us at great speed and lightning was already flashing across the valley beneath us. We immediately began to race back along the ridge and, conscious of our vulnerability as 'high spots' in an electrical storm, we searched desperately for a safe place to dive off the ridge. Eventually we shot down a scree slope for about 50 metres and then sat on our packs. By this time we were completely enveloped in cloud and heavy rain, we'd had no time to put on our waterproofs so we were soaked to the skin and, with the lightning flashing all around us, our metal buckles were humming with the electricity in the air. We sat shivering with the cold until the worst of the storm had passed. Then we got up, put our waterproofs on over our soaking wet clothes and set off to find shelter. We were fortunate that the incident had not been more serious because we had been complacent in not keeping a watchful eye on our environment.

IT'S A MATTER OF ATTITUDE

However prepared and equipped we try to be, we will never be able to prevent circumstances catching us unawares occasionally. Good preparation will inevitably stand us in good stead, but it is the attitude with which we handle issues that will define the kind of people we turn out to be. This Ella Wilcox poem sums it up beautifully:

The Winds of Fate
One ship bears East and another bears West
With the self same winds that blow,
But it's the set of the sails
Not the strength of the gales
That determine the ways we go.
Now the winds and the seas are the ways of fate
As we voyage along through life,
But it's the set of our soul
That determines our goal
Not the obstacles or the strife.

Adapted from "The Winds of Fate" by Ella Wheeler Wilcox
Published in 'The Best Loved Poems of the American People'
Garden City Books, New York, 1936.

As Christians, we must always be aware that however lovely our surroundings might be, the world we live in is a potentially hostile environment. What might appear to be calm and relaxing atmospheres around us can suddenly change into angry and threatening ones without warning. We must always be on our guard. Much of my early skiing experience was in Scotland where my friends and I learned very quickly that even on a beautiful sunny day with a perfectly clear sky, within a matter of 20 minutes, we could be engulfed in a raging blizzard where the temperature had dropped 20 degrees and visibility was down to zero. When I left school, my first job was in the housing department of the local authority and I remember one of the clerks, who was a Christian, trying to explain his faith to a fellow worker. His colleague listened intently for a while but then appeared to lose interest and mentally switched off. The Christian clearly didn't spot this so he carried on talking until suddenly the man exploded with very aggressive and abusive language. Everyone froze with shock, and a deathly silence descended over the office. The Christian was taken completely by surprise and beat an embarrassingly hasty retreat. He was just not aware of how the man's attitude was changing nor how the atmosphere in the room was shifting. I don't think he ever ventured into this man's territory again.

SENSITIVITY

We can all be guilty of not understanding our environment sufficiently so that, even when we are trying to be obedient to God's will, we can make some serious errors of judgement. These can leave us in a poor light with other people and can affect our desire to want to serve God in this way again. Furthermore, it can colour other people's thinking about God by leaving a negative impression of the way He loves us and cares about us. To serve God effectively therefore, requires us to be constantly attentive to the people and the environment in which He has placed us. Whether this is in the surroundings of our own home, in our neighbourhood, where we study or work, in a church setting or out on the street, we make ourselves vulnerable if we don't remain sensitive to the situations and circumstances around us at all times. This is not just about being observant, although this is a necessary skill, but it is about having open lines of communication with God to receive from Him information about what is happening in the spiritual realm. It is often easy to want to rely on our own experience but here our determination to look good can get in the way because it comes from our old nature. Sometimes we have to struggle to remain focused on the gentle promptings of The Holy Spirit so that we allow Him to speak into our regenerate nature. It is the attitude we show as we face each situation in life that will affect the outcome and will determine how much we can continue to move towards maturity.

Making a few simple, routine checks before setting out for a day's skiing is a very important habit to cultivate. There will be some important adjustments that need to be made between a day where the temperature is only just above freezing, compared to a day where it is around minus 30 degrees Celsius. When I was going through my BASI assessment programme, every one of the participants were expected to get up each morning in time to check the weather and snow reports for that day, to wax our own skis before breakfast, then to line up to have our skis inspected by the assessors, including being questioned about our choice of ski wax, and still be in the queue with our trainer to catch the ski lift as soon as it opened at 9.00am. It required a huge effort to maintain focus and get everything done in order to ensure that we didn't miss breakfast altogether. Great emphasis was placed on our ability to show that we were aware of how our environment was changing each day and whether we were quick enough and skilful enough to make the appropriate adjustments.

MAINTAINING FOCUS

On one occasion when I was attending the National Ski Areas of America conference in Steamboat Springs, Colorado, I had travelled up from Denver in a blizzard and my coach was the last to arrive before all roads to the resort were closed due to the heavy snow conditions. I woke early the next morning to see a beautifully clear sky and discover that over 3 feet (1 metre) of snow had fallen that night. I quickly found out that the conference was to be postponed for a couple of days to allow others caught in the snow, time to arrive. I was thrilled, and immediately put on my ski gear and rushed off to catch the first ski lift as soon as it opened. As I travelled up that first chairlift, I surveyed the beautiful pristine snow-covered ski runs and I decided to immediately catch another chairlift going higher, and then another one, until I reached the highest point in the resort at about 12,500 feet. I dismounted the chair and paused to take in the spectacular views all around me and to marvel at this opportunity to be among the first to ski the fresh snow on these runs. Eventually I set off with great excitement and skied about 250yards before screeching to a halt gasping for breath. My head was spinning, I wanted to vomit, my eyes had lost focus, my joints and muscles were aching, I was doubled up in pain and could barely stand. I remember praying to The Lord at this point saying "Lord, if you're going to take me now, you couldn't have chosen a better spot!" At that moment I was surrounded by perfect silence, there was no one else in view and I was convinced that I was going to die right there in the middle of the ski run. I must have been there for ages before it slowly began to dawn on me – I had travelled up from sea level to 12,500 feet in less than 24 hours – my body was suffering acute altitude sickness. In my great excitement at this unexpected opportunity to ski, I had completely overlooked the importance of sufficiently understanding my environment. I had ignored the need for my body to acclimatise at this altitude. If I had kept to my original intention, which was to enjoy some skiing at the end of the 4-day conference, I would probably have been fine, but allowing my enthusiasm to dictate my actions meant that I had not paid sufficient attention to my environment and this could have landed me in a very serious situation.

WALKING IN THE SPIRIT

I am conscious that there have been times in the past when I have done something similar in my enthusiastic attempts to serve The Lord. I have rushed ahead into situations which I thought I understood and in which I thought my experience would carry me through, only to discover that, because I wasn't fully aware of the environment at that moment, I had to make an embarrassingly quick exit. I am aware that it is just so easy to fall into this trap because our old nature is desperate to prove how competent we are but we need to remember that once we become born-again believers God gives us the ability to see everything in a different light. We are no longer merely physical beings, our spiritual dimension has been brought to life by the power of The Holy Spirit within us and we have been transformed into spiritual beings living within a physical body. Paul puts it this way, "For you were once darkness, but now you are light in The Lord. Live as children of light" (Ephesians 5 v 8). Learning to 'live as children of light' involves us walking daily with The Lord, in the light of His presence and being sensitive to His promptings. We should no longer be dominated by the workings of our old nature where our eyes get blinded, our ears get dulled and our minds get captivated by the physical world around us. We are entering a whole new world with new prospects and opportunities, but these can only be realised as we develop a greater and more accurate awareness of our environment and then face this by drawing on the wealth of resources God has made available to us.

THE RESORT

One of the nice things about planning a ski holiday is looking through the brochures at the wide choice of resorts and then selecting one that provides all the benefits of challenge and relaxation that you think will give you the most enjoyment. In making the final choice of resort, many factors need to be considered according to the preferences and ski experience of your party. The avid skiers will be looking for a wide choice of ski runs and ski lifts, whereas the not-so-proficient-skiers will be hoping for some gentle ski runs with lots of mountain cafes and restaurants, and the non-skiers will be looking for a range of shops and eating places along with some lovely walks and great après ski activities. Skiers will also tend to scrutinise the ski-lift maps to work out which runs will be available on their lift-pass and research possible links to other ski areas, whereas for others, the journey, how to get there and how long it will take, will be far more important. For the skiers, the height of the resort above sea-level and its snow record will be a most significant factor, so some detailed research will be necessary prior to making a decision. On one occasion I was involved with a party of around 140 people on a ski trip to the Black Forest area in Germany. Although the resort was quite low in altitude it was an ideal location for beginners because it was easily accessible and had a good record for early season snow. However, on this particular trip there wasn't a single snowflake in sight. We were able to sit on the grass in beautiful warm sunshine and gaze at the glaciers of Austria gleaming in the sun 50 miles away. It demonstrated the importance of doing some careful research before planning a trip even though there may be some who would be perfectly content to have good local facilities and be able to enjoy the beauty of the scenery in which the resort is set.

The ski chalet provides warmth and comfort after a day on the mountain

THE SPIRITUAL HOME

Working through the factors involved in choosing a ski resort draws my attention to how many aspects we ought to be taking into account when choosing a church to attend, which we may want to make our spiritual home. There are a number of things we may want and some things we almost certainly will need from a fellowship of believers, but people rarely seem to pay much attention to these things before taking the step of committing themselves to a church. We wouldn't be this casual with a holiday booking yet our spiritual health and enjoyment is so much more important. We might take into account the distance we need to travel, how we plan to get there and the timing of the meetings as fairly obvious factors, but the importance of being able to receive sound Biblical teaching and training on a consistent basis can be so easily overlooked. Then there is the element of our personal growth and development which only takes place when we are in an environment where we are encouraged to be actively using the skills, talents and abilities God has given us. Spiritual growth doesn't happen when we are static or backsliding in the Christian faith and that can only happen when any growth and development are absent. Like a ski resort, we want our spiritual home to be a place of active learning, friendship and fun. We should look to see if there is a range of possibilities in which we might want to be involved, and consider whether there are any exciting plans and proposals for the future. We will want to feel that we really belong in our chosen environment and that we can look forward to both fresh challenges and fresh opportunities every day.

THE HOTEL OR CHALET

The place where we choose to eat and sleep in a ski resort is a bit like a Christian home-group. We want to feel completely at home and very comfortable here. It should be a place where we can be ourselves without putting on any 'airs and graces' in front of others, a place where we feel able to share our experiences of the day including our successes and our failures, a place where we can learn from one another, a place of both giving and receiving, sharing advice and encouragement, a place to laugh and cry together. It should be a place of honesty where we can share our doubts and fears knowing that we will be heard sympathetically and that our aches and pains can receive the ministry they need. In the busy-ness and activity of the ski resort, there is generally no time to address personal issues so we can be left feeling rejected or unfulfilled. We need to be able to 'unload' with like-minded people in an atmosphere of confidentiality and mutual support.

The Christian homegroup needs to be a place where we can ask questions or challenge the views of other people, and where we learn to develop the spiritual skills God has given us by practicing on one another. If we cannot learn to minister to the people within our Christian circle, we will find it extremely hard to do this with people outside the church, yet this is where the real work is to be undertaken. The safety of the homegroup is where we can open The Word together, to discuss and debate how to put it into practice, to learn from those who are more experienced and to encourage those among us who may be timid and weak. We should not be worried about making mistakes but understand that we are in an environment where there are no 'experts' but that we are all willing to be learning from each other. This is where we learn the balance between boldness and sensitivity, where we allow everyone to express their point of view, where we grow most towards spiritual maturity, and where we learn to be more acutely aware of our environment. Every time we come out of our spiritual chalet, we should feel all fired up, raring to go, and ready to face the challenges of the world again.

No. 2 A typical view of beautiful snow-covered mountains

No. 3 A ski instructor explaining to his pupils the importance of developing good technique in the snowplough turns.

No. 6 A typical view looking down a 'blue' run and showing un-pisted areas at the side

No. 4 A close-up showing how the ski boots are held securely by the ski bindings

No. 5 A ski resort showing ski runs coming down into the villag

No. 7 A mogul field is created by the passage of many skiers down
an un-pisted slope

No. 8 A variety of ski lifts starting from a central location

No. 9 A ski instructor leading his class by demonstrating 'stem-christie' turns

No. 10 A downhill racer demonstrating dynamic balance in the turn

No. 11 A time-lapsed photograph of a skier doing parallel turns

No. 12 A mature skier gliding effortlessly through soft snow

No. 13 The author at the head of La Grande Motte glacier

Christian Parallels | PART 6

Reading the Terrain

I definitely inherited my love of the great outdoors from my mother who, when I was young, took me on frequent long walks in the countryside. My practical skills in lightweight camping, however, came from my time as a teenager in The Boys' Brigade. We regularly undertook Duke of Edinburgh Award expeditions and lightweight camping trips to many parts of the country but among the most memorable were those we enjoyed in the mountains of Wales. On one 3-day expedition we were crossing a large boggy area on route to the top of mount Snowdon when one of the less experienced lads in our group suddenly sank up to his waist. We laughed as we pulled him out because fortunately it was only his dignity that was hurt. As I remember this incident, an episode of the TV programme 'The Vicar of Dibley' springs into my mind. In this particular episode the vicar, Geraldine Grainger, and her man-friend were walking along a muddy track in the rain. She was trying to impress him with her joyful attitude by splashing through the mud until she finally jumped into a small puddle and sank up to her neck. My friends and I had spent quite a bit of time in wild country in Wales and in Scotland and we had learned to recognise how the different colours and types of the grasses and vegetation were an indication of how firm the ground would be underneath them. Consequently we had learned from experience which areas were most likely to provide a firm footing and those that were best avoided. For both the skier and the Christian, learning to accurately read the terrain is a sign of developing maturity and is a very important quality in terms of safety and survival.

THE SKI RUNS

The ski runs are the roadways of the skier. They are prepared routes which usually link to mountain cafes, restaurants and ski lifts. In most ski resorts, the ski runs are graded with an internationally accepted colour code to indicate the average gradient and level of difficulty, - Green, Blue, Red and Black – and are signed with numbered markers to indicate your proximity to the end of the run. Even allowing for this, there are many factors that can create massive differences and challenges that cannot always be predicted along the length of any ski run. For example, there can be enormous variations in the width of the run and it could include narrow tracks, paths or even roads. There are many different types of snow conditions to contend with, for example, soft, firm, hard, sugary, icy, crusty, deep, powder, slush and ice. Subtle changes in the gradient can easily throw people off balance. There will be hollows and holes, there will be humps, bumps and moguls, there could be obstacles of all kinds including rocks, trees, stumps, heather, streams, crevasses, drag lifts, piste grooming machines and other hazards, not to mention the most unpredictable of them all - other people ! In addition to all these, there can be sudden changes in the temperature - which could immediately affect the quality of the snow, changes in the weather - such as cloud or snow or blizzard, and changes in the quality of light from bright sunlight to flat light where it becomes impossible to distinguish bumps and hollows. Some of these changes can happen gradually whereas others can occur suddenly, but in all cases it will require the skier to make some subtle changes in technique to be able to manage them effectively. The main requirement here, initially, is to demonstrate keen powers of observation and recognise these hazards at the earliest opportunity, then have the wisdom and confidence to use the appropriate skills to overcome them or manage them. The ability to do this, as a skier, is a sign of growing maturity.

SPIRITUAL OBSTACLES

In the Christian life, the hazards and challenges are not quite so easily identified but one thing is certain, there will be masses of them. They will come in all shapes and sizes and frequently without any warning. Many of them will be impossible to accurately predict though some will be comparatively easy to spot in advance. However, to develop the range of skills required to cope with these, is a task which involves constant personal spiritual growth and development. For the Christian, relapse occurs when growth and development stop. To be committed to the task of keeping on growing and developing is a challenge in itself, but many people choose to relax and merely coast along in their faith, not realising that this can leave them vulnerable to being knocked sideways by one hazard or another. Some people will show real determination to overcome the obstacles in their life whereas others may allow themselves to drift along perhaps because they were not sufficiently warned about the dangers or because they are frightened by them. The only way we can be certain to cope with every hazard of life, regardless of where it originates, is to be daily walking in close relationship with Jesus. We can see that this has always been God's plan for us when we read, for example, the words of Psalm 23:

> *The Lord is my shepherd, I shall not be in want,*
> *He makes me lie down in green pastures,*
> *He leads me beside quiet waters, He restores my soul. He*
> *guides me in paths of righteousness for His name's sake.*
> *Even though I walk through the valley of the shadow of*
> *death, I will fear no evil for You are with me. Your rod and*
> *staff, they comfort me. You prepare a table before me in the*
> *presence of my enemies, You anoint my head with oil, my*
> *cup overflows. Surely goodness and love will follow me all*
> *the days of my life, And I will dwell in the house of The*
> *Lord for ever.*

> *(The New International Version)*

GOD'S PROVISION

There are a number of other Psalms which echo a similar theme and this is picked up throughout the New Testament, for example in 2 Peter 1 v 3 - 11. From these passages, we can clearly see that our struggle to grow towards maturity is not about trying to persuade God to do something for us, but is all about us being open to receive what He has already done for us. This doesn't sit well with our old unregenerate nature and so we are constantly tempted to return to our old ways of doing things and exercise our determination to demonstrate how independent we can be. What happens, as a consequence, is that we lose our ability to correctly interpret the world around us because we see it only through our own human eyes and this makes us vulnerable to being deceived by its hazards and schemes. This, in turn, robs us of our joy and makes our Christian life one of constant struggle and disappointment. We actually need God's perspective and His wisdom if we are to make sense of the world around us (Proverbs 4 v 1 - 11). The amazing thing is that God makes this freely available to us because Wisdom is one of the supernatural gifts of His Holy Spirit (1 Corinthians 12 v 8). God's plan therefore, is that we should be "more than conquerors" (Romans 8 v 37), and daily walk in victory through our Lord Jesus Christ (1 Corinthians 15 v 37). We should recognise too, that although all our talents, skills and abilities were given us by our creator God, the responsibility for developing them and using them rests firmly with us.

THE HOLY SPIRIT

To enable us to experience this victorious living on a daily basis, God has given us the supernatural gifts of His Holy Spirit so that we can approach every situation from a spiritual perspective and not simply rely on our past experiences or earthly wisdom. Receiving these gifts opens for us completely new levels of perception and understanding about the world around us. As we begin to exercise these gifts, it will cause us to wonder how on earth people manage to get through life without these amazing qualities. When Paul introduces these gifts to the Corinthian church, he says "Now about spiritual gifts, brothers, I do not want you to be ignorant" (1 Corinthians 12 v 1). He goes on to explain that these are given to strengthen and equip us so that we are better able to serve others in the process of helping to build the kingdom of God. They give us the ability to see things more accurately and then to make Godly choices about what to tackle, what to avoid, and how to move forward. However, our ability to help others is dependent upon recognising their <u>real</u> needs rather than; a) what we want to give them, or b) what we think they need, or even c) what they think they need.

I have witnessed many well-meaning Christians trying to help other people without making any attempt to discover what their real needs are. It is commendable for people to want to use their experiences of life to help others, but this, on its own, is old nature mentality and can come across as critical, judgemental and dictatorial. Furthermore, It demonstrates an inaccurate 'reading of the terrain' and can increase the likelihood of frustration and failure on the part of the hearers. We can easily fall into the trap of telling others what they should be doing, or simply giving advice, instead of helping people explore and learn how to listen, to hear, and to obey God for themselves. I have heard many well-meaning skiers telling others what they should be doing without realising they are merely helping people reproduce their own faults. Lots of people, both Christian and non-Christian, consider themselves to be 'counsellors' without ever having understood the basic skills required for this role. They are often, quite unintentionally, creating more problems than they are trying to resolve because they don't spend sufficient time listening. Even secular models of problem management include, as a first step, the importance of accurately understanding the situation as it actually exists before starting to consider possible solutions. I am a great believer in Counselling, and that it is a Christian prerogative, but I have serious concerns about people who undertake this without formal training. I hold the same opinion whether speaking about a Counsellor, about a Christian, or about a Skier – beware of old nature mentality, it can do more harm than good and frequently prevents us from accurately reading the terrain.

GOING OFF–PISTE

Many skiers love the idea of going off-piste to make their own tracks in untouched powder snow. The piste, relates to those areas of snow that have been compacted by a piste-grooming machine. These machines help to keep the snow in place by compressing it a little and this prevents it from being blown away by the wind or swept away by the traffic of skiers. By definition therefore, 'off-piste' relates to those areas that have not been groomed in this way and which can often include areas of deep powder snow which require a quite different technique. Such areas also do not have the benefit of convenient restaurants, sign posts or ski patrols. Alongside the edges of the piste there will often be areas of soft snow the piste machines haven't touched, but the term off-piste usually refers to whole areas of the mountain where there has been no traffic of any sort. These areas usually don't start or end near the ski lifts and can be quite isolated so may be difficult to get to and to come away from. Anyone contemplating an off-piste adventure should always go with a group of skiers and preferably with an experienced ski guide. They should be sure to let others know where they are going and the time at which they anticipate returning. To be able to read the terrain accurately when going

Piste-grooming machines compact the snow which clearly defines the ski runs.

off-piste is a skill that requires local knowledge as well as skiing and mountain experience. People who have grown up in a particular locality will possess a level of understanding that visitors to the area will not have and their expertise could be a major factor in the safe enjoyment of the ski party. Going into unfamiliar territory on your own should never be considered, either for a skier or a Christian.

UNCHARTED TERRITORY

In the early days of learning to walk by faith, Christians would do well to keep to the tried and tested pathways of activity and service. However, there is a balance to be maintained here. Every believer, at some point, will find themselves exposed to a situation that is completely unfamiliar to them. God often seems to delight in putting people into situations that are outside their comfort zone so they will realise that they simply have to call on His resources rather than try to cope on their own. We shouldn't be worried by this because He sees this as a necessary part of our spiritual development. It is in these situations that we need to rely on our supernatural guide – The Holy Spirit, but our failure to do this will only result in making the issues more difficult for us than they need be. There is also a great difference between finding ourselves in a situation which God has engineered for us, as opposed to deliberately venturing into areas of our own choosing. The former will help us mature whereas the latter will demonstrate great immaturity. We must all work at improving our levels of sensitivity to God's promptings because, regardless of our circumstances, He alone enables us to read the terrain accurately. Immersing ourselves in regular and detailed study of the Scriptures is a vital part of this process. God will sometimes put people alongside us to provide encouragement and help with our understanding, but at other times we may appear to be isolated with only His presence and the knowledge of His Word for comfort. The body of believers in which we fellowship, the church, is meant to be a safe place for us to develop these skills before venturing into the outside world. It should also be a safe place to come back to and share our successes and our failures in an atmosphere of mutual learning. We never get to the end of this learning cycle. God's desire is to continually refine us, strengthen us and equip us for what He has next and, because there are always new situations and circumstances for us to face, He wants us to get better at reading the terrain.

AVALANCHES

One of the most devastating and destructive things about not accurately reading the terrain in an off-piste ski area is the potential danger of an avalanche. Avalanches can be triggered in several ways but are usually the result of a change in air temperature which subsequently causes one layer of snowfall to slide across another layer and crash down the mountain. They have immense power and are capable of sweeping away trees and buildings in their path often reaching speeds in excess of 200mph. When people are caught in an avalanche they are churned up with the accumulated ice blocks and other debris which makes their chances of survival very low. People will often be injured and buried when the snow finally comes to a halt so immediate search and rescue is of paramount importance. Many will suffer panic attacks whilst struggling with the intense cold and at the same time often enduring a limited air supply.

When I was taking part in my ski coaches training course in 1979, one of the subjects on the programme was 'developing a better understanding of avalanche issues'. As a means of appreciating one aspect of what people experience when caught in an avalanche, the trainers explained that they had dug a deep hole in the snow and would be asking us individually if we were willing to lay in the bottom while they filled it in. To give us a real life experience of what it is like to be buried, the plan was that they would leave us for 20 minutes before coming back to dig us out. The tension in the group was unbelievable. I watched the colour draining out of people's faces as one by one we were put on the spot. When it was my turn, I lay in the bottom of the hole, put one hand over my mouth to help my breathing and waited as the weight of the snow was shovelled on top of me. The first few minutes weren't too bad except for feeling totally pinned down and unable to move in any way. Then the feelings of panic began to rise. They started in my stomach and gradually increased as they moved towards my throat. I wanted to scream, but by the grace of God I was able to bring the feelings under control. I was so grateful when I heard the team starting to dig me out, and when I finally surfaced I actually wanted to hug those guys even though I had only been under the snow for a few minutes. It was an experience that took me back to my caving days when I remember a friend being stuck underground and unable to move for a while. I never want to repeat the exercise but it gave me just a tiny appreciation of what people may suffer when buried in snow or caught in an avalanche.

FEAR PARALYSES

Over the years, I have worked with quite a number of people who have described their situation to me as if they have been caught in an avalanche. People have said they feel trapped, unable to breathe, oppressed, weighed down, unable to move, completely isolated with no-one to help, unable to think straight, often unable even to call for help and experiencing feelings of panic on a regular basis. The Bible tells us that our enemy, the devil, is constantly looking for people devour (1 Peter 5 v 8), and his strategy is to steal, kill and destroy (John 10 v 10). Furthermore, he wants to paralyse us with fear so that we will be unable to move, in the spiritual realm. In such a situation it is easy to see how hope can quickly disappear and leave people feeling abandoned and helpless. We are living in a world which is dominated by violence and fear where it is common for people to feel trapped and without hope. This kind of fear seems to prevent people from responding in the way they might do normally and prompts them to want to withdraw and hide away. When this happens to us as Christians, it becomes impossible for us to function effectively and we become vulnerable to whatever the world throws at us. Instead, we must learn to call on the resources of Almighty God to help us cope with the situation. He often will not take the situation away but will give us what we need to be able to manage it more effectively. He can make it possible for us to experience victory in His name even when the situation seems impossible from a human point of view. When we begin to see every situation, whether good, bad or indifferent, as a potential for our growth and development in the Christian faith, we are well on our way to achieving new levels of spiritual maturity.

THE SKILL REQUIRED

By far the most important aspect here is to develop our ability to accurately read the terrain so that we can avoid at least some of those areas which are prone to spiritual avalanches or other hazards. Learning to spot danger areas is not just a safety element for ourselves, but is about being a good example to those around us. This is not a hard or rigid interpretation of our surroundings because we recognise that they can change so quickly. What may be perfectly safe one day can become a major hazard on another day. Reading the terrain is about exercising good judgement and this is the correct application of knowledge at any given point in time. It is what we might refer to as Wisdom, and The Bible speaks at great length about its importance to us (James 3 v 13 - 18). As a skier, learning to read the terrain is an essential quality for our own safety and protection but, although this is also true for us as Christians, it is a necessary skill that will make all the difference in our effectiveness for the kingdom of God. In those businesses where the sales assistants are trained, they are taught to carefully watch and listen to their clients so that they can identify people who are simply interested to browse the merchandise. They are then taught to notice the subtle changes in their behaviour that indicate a specific interest in a product, because this dramatically increases the likelihood of being able to make a sale. They are taught to 'read the terrain'. If we can learn, develop and refine this skill as Christians, we will find that our witness to people all around us will become so much more powerful and effective. It is not so much about what we are able to offer, or about bringing people to where we are, but about meeting the needs of people where they are.

THE MOGUL FIELD

There is a big difference between being able to cruise down a wide, pisted ski run, and being able to successfully master a mogul field. Moguls are created by the passage of many skiers over an un-pisted slope, so that large bumps of firm snow get formed that can look, from a distance, a bit like a sheet of bubble-wrap. For the novice skier, this can present a huge challenge because the bumps make turning the skis more of a challenge and keeping dynamic balance becomes a major exercise. It is as though the terrain is now dictating where and when you can make a turn. This means that much more flexibility and speed of movement is required from your knees and legs so that your upper body can remain calm and balanced at all times. We live in a world that is continually being cut and shaped by the passage of many people, and this is creating huge bumps and hollows for us to negotiate as Christians. In every area of life standards are being eroded, laws are being passed, and opinions and values are being shaped by the volume of the popular opinion of the moment. What is being taught in our schools and colleges can be of great concern for young people, and what is being broadcast across all aspects of the media can create massive areas of potential conflict and anxiety for every believer. In an attempt to pacify the masses, (that is those who seem to shout the loudest), the whole of society appears to be moving further and further away from the standards of The Bible. In education, in business, in sport, socially, and even in the family, Christians are being put under pressure to accept and conform to worldly standards. Such tension has the tendency to throw us off balance, spiritually, and this can cause us to be more concerned about how we are perceived by others and to focus more on the problems than on the solutions. As soon as we are made to feel inferior to our surroundings, we have an automatic tendency to succumb to them (Matthew 14 v 29- 30). Unfortunately, we only get stronger in our faith as we choose to rise to the occasion and face such challenges. A delicate balance is required here if we are to maintain our faith (and credibility) without becoming dogmatic about what we believe or judgemental and critical about what others believe. We must be most sensitive, not only to the way we respond, but to the timing of our responses. In addition, we must be aware of whether our lifestyle matches what we say. Someone has said "What you are shouts so loud that people can't hear what you say".

Christian Parallels | PART 7

Mastering Moving Upwards

Getting to the top of the mountain has always been a target for experienced skiers. In the early days people had to climb up through the snow whilst carrying their skis on their backs. I remember one old skier in the Cairngorms telling me that he would spend over 6 hours climbing in one day to get just 6 minutes of skiing. Even today people will undertake hours of serious climbing to get to areas of untouched powder snow on fresh slopes. However, most ski resorts now have a variety of modern forms of transport that make it really easy to get

A button lift pulls skiers to the top of the ski run

to high places in the mountains. Oddly though, this can also present a very real danger because it makes it easy for people who are not properly equipped or prepared for high altitudes to reach places that would otherwise be inaccessible to them.

There are a whole variety of systems that are used in ski resorts to transport people to high places in the mountains. Some of these require people to be wearing their skis, whereas others can be accessed by people whether they are skiers or not. In order to grow towards spiritual maturity we will need to move higher in our relationship with The Lord and we could encounter a variety of ways in which we are encouraged to do this. The main types of ski lifts fall into the following categories:

i. A Rope Drag Lift. This is simply a moving rope which you grip with your hands and allow yourself to be dragged up the slope while trying to keep in balance on your skis. It is not unusual in the Christian faith to know that there are occasions when we feel we are simply hanging on and being dragged along while trying desperately to maintain some kind of balance. This can be hard work at the time but, in hindsight, we may realise that it has produced some good learning opportunities for us and, at the same time, it may have actually strengthened our grip on some spiritual matters.

ii. A Conveyor Belt. This is usually a constantly moving rubber mat which you stand on while wearing your skis, allowing it to carry you up the slope. There will be times in the Christian life when we need to be carried along by others even though we may feel capable of doing things in our own strength. This can help take the strain out of some of our early learning experiences, but it is essential that we quickly learn how to move on from this.

iii. A Button Tow. Here you are required to grab a metal bar with a button on the end of it and thrust it between your legs so that it pulls you up the slope whilst standing on your skis. You are literally being pulled up by the seat of your pants! Some of these bars may be fixed to an overhead cable and therefore are constantly moving, whereas others slide onto a moving overhead cable once you have grabbed the bar. The important thing here is to stand firmly on your feet and push them forward slightly while keeping your knees well flexed to absorb any bumps or jolts. Some people, if they are not ready, have been pulled off their feet by the bar while others who try to sit on the button will fall over backwards. A Christian will often be required to go with something that is already moving or to take hold of something that is about to move. We should be careful not to be taken by surprise when something takes off quickly, and not be overwhelmed by it. We also should not fall into the trap of trying to resist progress nor try to sit firmly where we are so that we fall down backwards. Maintaining dynamic balance is the essence at all times.

iv.   A 'T' Bar Tow. These can be quite challenging to negotiate since they involve two people grabbing a 'T' shaped bar between them so that they can be pulled up the slope on their skis side by side. To be able to negotiate this successfully, there must be an attitude of equality between the two people to ensure that one person doesn't push the other one off. It involves mutual trust, without losing individual focus, to work together and support each other throughout the journey. We are sometimes called to work alongside another person in the Christian faith and therefore need to develop that sense of mutual trust and sharing without either person losing their balance or trying to dominate the other person.

All the above forms of uplift involve skiers standing on their own two feet and maintaining their balance while being transported up the hill. As we move towards spiritual maturity, every Christian should seek to develop their faith in ways which will allow them to be drawn higher in their relationship to God. This involves being able to stand securely and hold on, with good balance while God provides the momentum.

The following types of lifts all differ from the previous ones in that they require people to completely surrender their control and trust themselves unreservedly to the transport which will carry them high up into the mountains. Some of these lifts can also be used by non-skiers who wish to enjoy the stunning scenery of the higher mountains.

v.   A Chair Lift. The chairs are usually fixed to a moving cable. This requires you to get into position so that as the chair arrives it will scoop you up and carry you up the mountain. Chairs can be for almost any number of people and have a safety bar that is brought down once everyone is seated. Skiers keep their skis on throughout this journey in order to be able to ski off at the arrival point whilst the chair continues on its way. To be carried along, and therefore relinquish control in this manner, contains its own anxieties, but it has its rewards of being able to see things from quite a different perspective. On most chairlifts the skiers remain open to the elements, so wearing well insulated clothing is essential. Care should be taken not to drop anything during the ride because the route will often cross some fairly inaccessible places. For the Christian, the concept of being carried by God over difficult terrain is an example of His divine love, protection and care (Deuteronomy 1 v 32), but the requirement to surrender control can still be quite a daunting experience for some. We are also told in the New Testament that "men spoke from God as they were carried along by The Holy Spirit" (1 Peter 1 v 21). We can be assured that we will always reach new levels of spiritual awareness when we allow The Holy Spirit to carry us, but we must be ready.

vi.   A Gondola. These are little cabins that generally hold 2, 4, 6, or 8 people and usually carry skiers to higher places, often over longer distances. People put their skis in a container on the outside and then jump inside while the cabin moves slowly past them. It then slides down onto a moving cable as the doors close automatically. Being seated inside a cabin means that you are protected from the weather and have the opportunity to socialise with others during the journey. The Christian journey is so much more meaningful when it is not made in isolation, but with other like-minded individuals. As we journey together towards new spiritual heights, it is a joy to be able to share this with other people and know that we are being held securely and safely within the protection God is providing for us. Gondolas can carry people who are vastly different in their levels of ability and understanding.

vii.   A Cable Car. These are usually much bigger cabins which may hold up to 120 people at a time and are counter-balanced by two cars moving in opposite directions. People can walk into them with, or without their skis and be whisked up the mountain at high speed. Standing in close proximity to a large number of people can be a bit stressful for some, but thoughts of the eventual destination usually keep everyone in a positive mood. Christians are part of a large body of people God is moving into new levels of relationship by His Holy Spirit. For some people, this can be a strange, high speed spiritual experience which takes them into unfamiliar territory at high altitude. The rewards, however, can be spectacular and breath-taking.

viii.   A Funicular. This is a railway-type vehicle which is pulled by a cable on a cogged track and is balanced by two cars moving in opposite directions. It can be used by skiers, non-skiers, and sightseers alike and is a railway that usually runs up steep gradients, often through tunnels in the mountains. There almost certainly will be times in the journey of a Christian when everything appears dark and any form of vision appears to be impossible. When the way ahead appears closed in and any view to the sides is blocked, we may be experiencing one of those tunnel-like periods in life. These are times when we learn to trust God completely. Even when we cannot see a light at the end of the tunnel, we have the certainty of knowing that we are in the hands of Almighty God and that He will bring us safely to our destination.

ix.   A Helicopter. Really adventurous and competent skiers may hire a helicopter to transport them to otherwise inaccessible slopes and off-piste runs. The experience of being whizzed up into the air and carried over amazing scenery is thrilling, but to then be put down onto untouched snow slopes and have the opportunity to lay down the first ski tracks, is beyond exciting. As Christians we are sometimes given the opportunity to break new ground in the spiritual realm. God can lift us supernaturally in the spirit and enable us to see things of which others are not aware and then experience the thrills of walking with Him along uncharted pathways. He may want us to pioneer new opportunities or to carve out new avenues of service. His supernatural gifts have already been made available to us so that we might be the vessels who can bring the amazing power of the living God directly into the lives of other people.

FEAR OF HEIGHTS

The Bible tells us that God has raised us up and seated us with Him in the heavenly realms, far above the physical and practical workings of the world (Ephesians 2 v 6). His purpose is that we should see things from His spiritual perspective (from above), instead of from our earthly, horizontal, worldly perspective. Unfortunately there are things that can get in our way and prevent us seeing God's point of view. I have encountered many people who have been absolutely terrified at the prospect of having to get on any form of ski lift – whether a chairlift, a gondola or a cable car. I have also worked with a lot of people who were not afraid of the lifts, but were terrified of coming down the ski slope once they had disembarked at the top. Such feelings would inevitably ruin a holiday for most people and could be quite upsetting for others in their party. I can certainly understand that people may look at these 'tin-cans-on-a-string' and see something very fragile and unstable which can stir up within them strong feelings of fear and vulnerability.

There are many Christians who experience very similar fearful feelings regarding issues around understanding and moving in the things of The Holy Spirit. Such feelings are frequently exacerbated by stories they have heard about crazy people doing crazy things in the name of Holy Spirit while supposedly under His influence. People will, understandably, be hesitant about relinquishing their control under these circumstances so it is essential that they are properly informed from what The Bible has to say about these matters rather than listening to the gossip of the moment. There is no doubt that learning to move in the spiritual realm can be open to misinterpretation and misunderstanding, but that is no reason for us to overlook this vital aspect of the Christian life. In fact, it is all the more reason for us to look at this issue carefully and from a Biblical point of view. The reality is that we are all spiritual beings, living temporarily in a physical body. The Bible makes it clear that everything we experience during our time in this physical body is a preparation for what God has in store for us in our spiritual future. Therefore, since every aspect of Christianity relates to the spiritual realm rather than simply the physical, and God wants us to begin to see things from His perspective, we should ask The Holy Spirit to give us a clear understanding of these things (1 Corinthians 2 v 12 - 14).

There is a kind of fear that can paralyse us, like a rabbit in the headlights of an oncoming car, but the Bible tells us that God's perfect love will drive all fear from us (1 John 4 v 16 - 18). We can make this true for ourselves as we choose to focus on the promises God has given us, as revealed in The Bible, and step out in faith by taking Him at His word. Sometimes we will need the encouragement of another believer to help us see in the spiritual realm instead of simply going along with what we see in front of us in the physical realm alone. I have often encouraged people to ride up ski tows or travel in gondolas and cable cars while singing out loud -"In the name of Jesus we have the victory". I have also encouraged many people to sing choruses out loud as they ski down the slopes. This is a process of occupying the mind with something positive so that it has little time to focus on anything negative. This psychological approach of focusing the mind is often used to help people who experience panic attacks, so that, with practice, they can banish all fears from their minds (Psalm 23 v 4). Many Christians have also benefitted from developing the skill of meditating on the Scriptures to achieve a similar result.

REACHING NEW HEIGHTS

As mentioned earlier, we understand that God has already blessed in a spiritual sense, us by raising us up to great heights to be seated with Him in the heavenly realms (Ephesians 1 v 3, and Ephesians 2 v 6). It is here that God's desire is for us to demonstrate His supernatural power to the spirit world (Ephesians 3 v 10). Our real battle, therefore, is not in the physical realm but in the spiritual realm (Ephesians 6 v 12), and we are equipped for this through the provision of God's supernatural power and authority (Colossians 2 v 10) which He has made available to us. We cannot battle against spiritual forces in a physical manner, however hard we try, but we must learn to utilise our spiritual heritage (2Corinthians 10 v 3 - 4). This is not purely about overcoming our fears but about beginning to see that we have a role to play in a whole new dimension. Although we will now be facing some spiritual battles, learning to live and move as spiritual beings will also open up to us new opportunities that we never thought possible before. We will begin to be sensitive to things in the spiritual realm that we would never have been aware of through our physical senses alone. We will begin to view everything differently and will develop a genuine excitement about moving and operating within this new lifestyle. Furthermore, as long as we maintain our focus on Him, all our fear and anxiety will disappear and we can react using the spiritual strength God provides. As soon as we are distracted by the physical world around us, just like Peter on lake Galilee, we will start to sink (Matthew 14 v 30). From our new position, seated with Christ in the heavenly realms, we have the possibility of seeing God's plans and purposes more clearly. We can begin to see that He really is in control and that whatever happens in the physical realm, God is able to use to bring about His purposes in the spiritual realm, through us.

Christian Parallels | PART 8

Developing Specific Skills

T he secret ingredient to having the most exciting and exhilarating times on skis is to develop the necessary skills to be able to negotiate any slope with confidence and ease, at any time, regardless of the conditions. Every activity or sport requires a certain level of skill to be able to take part successfully (and safely), and to achieve some desirable goals. Living the Christian life is no different. Unfortunately many Christians believe that once they have taken the step to follow Jesus, no further action is required, in fact, many people are actually told this by prominent people in the church. When this happens, without realising it, people can be lulled into a state of inactivity that leaves them vulnerable to the attacks of the enemy. Whilst there are very definitely things we should not be doing in the Christian life, there are lots of things where God has put the ball firmly in our court and is waiting to see how we respond. If we fail to take up this challenge, we will find ourselves drifting or stagnating, from a spiritual point of view, and our lives will become unnecessarily routine and boring. I have heard many people say that Christianity doesn't work for them, or that God has not proved Himself to them, yet when I have challenged them to explain this, I can tell that they have never been able to completely surrender themselves to Him and therefore have not been able to develop their relationship with Him in a powerful way. Usually they have been trying to carry on with their life as if nothing had altered. There are no two ways about this, anyone who comes to Christianity (or to skiing) without being willing to dramatically change the way they think and act will be setting themselves up for disappointment and failure at every stage. Learning a new range of skills is a vital part of moving into this new style of being, and is an absolutely necessary part of the journey towards maturity.

When I was being assessed for my BASI qualification, my trainer took a group of us, about 10 in all, and told us that we would be assessed, not just on our skiing ability, but on our ability to describe and explain each ski movement accurately. During one indoor session when he proposed to put us to the test, he said to us, "The best way to do this is just to close your eyes and picture yourself performing the movement as you describe it". We were all feeling uncomfortable and very self conscious so we persuaded him to give us a demonstration. While he sat in deep concentration describing his chosen movement with his eyes closed, we all tip-toed out of the room. Fortunately he was able to see the funny side of this and it lightened the mood of the moment for us. I hope you won't be tempted to put down the book at this point and tip-toe out of the room, because I now want to describe to you some of the important elements of learning to ski, without the benefit of being able to demonstrate them.

To maintain dynamic balance a skier must remain at 90 degrees to their skis regardless of the steepness of the gradient.

DYNAMIC BALANCE

What may, at first sight, appear to be blatantly obvious, is the fact that all the skills of skiing are based around the importance of maintaining good balance. Unfortunately, for the novice, our understanding of balance is based on having something solid and immovable as a base, from which we can generate possible movement. Having both feet firmly on the ground would be a usual starting point for us, or keeping one foot static while we move the other one to a new position, like walking. It can therefore be quite unnerving to be expected to develop good balance – while both feet are sliding ! Coming to terms with this is where the exhilaration in skiing begins. This is known as 'dynamic balance' and it has to be continually adjusted according to the speed and the circumstances under which the feet are sliding. In order to maintain dynamic balance when skiing, as a general guide, the body should be kept roughly perpendicular (that is, at 90%) to the skis and to the angle of the slope, at all times, and not vertical, except when stationary and on flat ground. To illustrate this, try to imagine a skier moving down a steeply inclined ski slope. If he adopts a static form of balance, his body will be vertical while his skis are sloping downwards. This will put his weight firmly onto the back of his skis and give him no control whatsoever. In order to maintain control he must adopt a posture of dynamic balance where his body is perpendicular (at a right-angle) to his skis, even though his brain may be telling him that he is leaning forward unnaturally. Whilst perpendicular to the skis, the ankles, knees and hips must all be kept flexed to absorb any shocks and to keep a low centre of gravity. The arms should be spread slightly outwards with hands held slightly forward and the upper body tilted forward from the waist. The pelvis should be pushed forward to increase flexibility in the legs, and the head should be held up with eyes looking forward focussing on the terrain ahead. This will enable the whole body to be kept in a position of balanced anticipation and readiness.

THE DYNAMIC CHRISTIAN

Any person who is taking their first steps in the Christian life will need to learn how to trust God in ways that they have never previously experienced. Initially, this may feel quite unnatural and can create some internal struggles that never completely go away, but it is possible to gradually get better at this (Romans 7 v 15 - 25). To be able to move into, and grow, in the spiritual realm it really is necessary to move away from our previously learned static (worldly) ways of doing things and develop a new dynamic relationship with God. This is like learning to keep our balance whilst being aware that everything around us is constantly changing and that we are continually moving. It is here that we learn to build our trust in the things God has provided for us, even when our earthly nature is telling us otherwise (1 Corinthians 2 v 12 - 14). We must develop a different type of awareness with an ability to be constantly alert to what is happening around us in the spiritual realm. Without this dynamic element, our relationship with The Lord will only ever be a static one where we are continually trying to keep our lives under our own control, based on the physical information we are receiving through our senses. We all possess a fierce level of independence which means we continually strive to show that we just don't need to depend on anyone else, even God. It is almost as though we are saying to God, "I just can't trust you" and, "I really do know what is best for me". If we adopt this attitude it will cause our spiritual potential to stagnate and will prevent us from growing or moving towards maturity.

THE CORRECT USE OF SKI POLES

In the first few days of learning to ski, if we are not careful, two of the greatest hindrances will be our own ski poles. They can be a great asset, but we must quickly learn how to use them correctly if we are to prevent them from becoming a major distraction. The problem here is that we will be tempted to lean on them or rely on them at times when we actually need to be feeling our weight pressing down through our feet. Leaning and relying on our ski poles can therefore keep us off balance instead of improving our balance. In fact, as a general principle in skiing, any form of leaning is going to be counter-productive as we begin our journey towards skiing competence. It is essential that we learn at an early stage to dispense with anything that might hinder the development of our dynamic balance. Therefore lots of early activities on skis are best done without the use of our ski poles wherever possible. In this way we will learn more quickly to feel how our feet are able to maintain our balance and control our skis most effectively.

We saw earlier how our ski poles can be likened to our Christian friends and how they can be most helpful to us at certain times. However, we must recognise that they can also become a major distraction for us by getting us into some bad habits that will be extremely difficult to break at a later stage. Sometimes, with the best of intentions, our friends can prevent us from standing firmly on our own feet and from developing and maintaining our own spiritual dynamic balance. Their desire to be of help can occasionally become a hindrance because, with the best of intentions, they can encourage us to rely on them instead of learning to rely on God. We, in turn, must be careful not to fall into the same trap when we seek to help others who may be in need. We must not allow our own ego to get in the way by encouraging people to rely on us when they should be developing their own faith skills.

BEGINNING TO MOVE

Our first steps on skis will usually involve learning to slide them along on flat ground and beginning to change direction by stepping the heels around while keeping the front tips on the ground. Next, we learn to sidestep up a shallow gradient by digging in the ski edges and then turning on a shallow slope to slide gently down. These 'baby steps' are important in helping us become familiar with our new role as a completely different 'being', but immediately we are faced with a challenge, if we are to maintain our balance through these exercises, we will need to adopt some unfamiliar body positions. We are encouraged at all times to 'feel' through our feet and develop that sense of standing securely by allowing the skis to fully support us. Any leaning, either to the right or to the left, will cause us to overbalance only to discover that this cannot be corrected in ways we have used in the past.

The new Christian will face many similar kinds of challenges in learning how to stand securely in the strength God provides instead of relying on the strategies of the old nature. Learning to 'feel' the security of The Lord begins as we learn to put our faith in the facts as recorded in The Bible. When we look for the feelings first, we will invariably be disappointed. Any new-found Christian balance and poise we may acquire will only come with much practice and, like a novice skier, we are likely to wobble often, make mistakes frequently and trip ourselves up repeatedly. We shouldn't be in the least bit fazed by any of this because it is all a perfectly normal introduction to our development into becoming a completely different being.

The snowplough is an excellent basic skill from which to develop more advanced ski turns.

THE SNOWPLOUGH POSITION

Continuing progress into skiing will now involve learning to slide down gentle gradients and controlling the speed while keeping in dynamic balance. The most effective way of doing this is to use the 'snowplough' technique. This involves holding the skis in a 'V' shape with the tips close together and the heels pushed apart, keeping an equal amount of pressure in the centre of each ski while the skier faces straight downhill. As the skis are pushed apart each one automatically angles onto its inside edge and digs into the snow creating some resistance. This resistance can be increased or decreased by pushing the feet further apart, or relaxing a little and allowing them to come closer together. As long as the person's weight remains equally distributed, the skier will slide straight ahead with both skis skidding down the slope like a snowplough. The resistance created by each ski will be cancelled out by the other, and enable the skier to slide downhill in a straight line. This 'straight line' is referred to as 'the fall line'. It is the path a ball would take if it rolled slowly down the slope following the contours of the slope by the shortest possible route. Relaxing or softening the edges and bringing the feet closer together will allow the skis to pick up speed, whereas accentuating the edges (digging them into the snow) will increase the resistance and reduce the speed. All this is done with flexed knees pressing forward along the line of the ski to absorb any bumps or undulations whilst keeping pressure, through the toes, onto the centre of each ski equally. Dynamic balance is maintained by not leaning back or leaning to either side but by tipping the upper body forward slightly in an attitude of anticipation.

MAINTAINING CONTROL

Learning to control our speed and direction as a Christian is actually a delicate balance between exercising our own ability and allowing God to do it for us. If we choose to lean in either direction to the expense of the other, we risk getting things terribly wrong so they won't seem to work for us. Whilst God allows us to make our own choices, He wants us to use the spiritual qualities He has given us rather than rely solely on our human abilities. Just like the snowplough position, we are likely to get this right, only by trial and error, because most of us have a natural tendency to put more faith in one foot than the other. We trust what has worked for us in the past so will struggle with the concept, first of all, of standing firmly balanced on the Word of God. Then, once this has been achieved, we will grapple with the idea of surrendering our talents, gifts and skills to The Lord so that these can be empowered by Him to make us effective in the work of His kingdom.

EQUAL PRESSURE

To grow towards maturity in the Christian life it is vitally important to be able to maintain dynamic balance that is, remaining balanced while we are continually on the move. This involves holding, what appear to be, diametrically opposed spiritual principles in balance so that we can keep moving ahead smoothly. For example: it is vital to accept that when Jesus walked the earth He was 100% man and 100% God. The mathematics don't compute for us from a human point of view, but if you believe that He was either one or the other you are only partially correct and will end up in error. We must hold both of these truths in balance if we are to have any chance of growing towards spiritual maturity. Jesus said the road to Life is a narrow one and few people find it (Matthew 7 v 13 – 14). It could be described as a 'tightrope', or a very narrow road which, to walk it, requires extremely good balance. The thing about a tightrope is that without good balance, it is just as easy to fall off to the left as it is to fall off to the right so, as a Christian, beginning to lean in either direction is likely to drive us into error. Another issue we may struggle with is the concept of God's love and God's justice. We can only fully appreciate either of these when we see it within the context of the other. If we try to understand either one to the exclusion of the other, we will end up with an inaccurate understanding of both. As a general principle within Christianity, The Bible makes it clear that everything should be kept in balance. The chances are that anything which takes us to an extreme is likely to lead us into error. So anything on which we choose to put an unnecessary emphasis, especially at the expense of another principle, is going to lead us towards error (Ecclesiastes 7 v 18). This is a vital skiing principle - if we start to lean in any direction, we are likely to quickly lose our balance and be heading for a fall.

THE PRINCIPLES OF TURNING

As soon as we have mastered how to control our skis in a straight line, we need to learn how to use this skill to change direction (make turns) in order to avoid obstacles. It will be helpful for us at this point to understand that there are several important principles which apply to every turn we choose to make on skis, and all of them include the necessity of maintaining dynamic balance at all times. The four factors inherent in every ski turn can be remembered with the simple acrostic P.E.T.S., which stands for - Pressing, Edging, Turning, and Speed. Every turn requires each of these to be present in some measure and at some point, so if one or more of these is missing, the chances are that the turn simply won't happen but the energy expended will often result in the person falling over. When my wife had her initial introduction to skiing she couldn't understand why her skis just would not respond to her. She gritted her teeth, tensed every muscle, and shouted at them loudly, but they always seemed to go off in a direction of their own. She desperately wanted them to respond to thought transference or even verbal admonition, but unfortunately ski design hasn't reached that level yet. Skis are made to respond to the following factors:

Pressing: Skis are designed to respond to pressure, and pressure is exerted by pushing the shins forward in the ski boots and pressing down on the ball of the foot in the centre of the ski. This aims to bring the whole length of the ski into contact with the snow.

Edging: This occurs when a ski is angled against the snow by pushing it slightly away from the body. This causes the metal edge to dig into the snow and create a tiny platform along which the ski can slide.

Turning: A ski can most easily be turned when it is flat on the snow and when the weight of the person is in the centre of the ski, rather than when it is on its edge. Turning a ski is achieved by using the leverage of the bent lower leg and twisting the leg around the ball of the foot – in the way you might want to stub out a cigarette butt.

Speed: Some ski turns can only be performed when there is sufficient momentum to carry the skier through the movement phase without coming to a standstill. Most turns, however, can be performed at fairly slow speeds. Learning accurate movements at slow speeds will generally help to develop good technique and is a way of preventing bad habits that otherwise are likely to develop at higher speeds.

In addition to these factors, it is essential for dynamic balance to be maintained throughout every turn and this can be achieved by keeping the weight on the toes, keeping the knees flexed forward, keeping the upper body tilted forward slightly from the waist and holding the hands forward and wide. It will not be possible to maintain dynamic balance if the skier stands too upright, leans back, begins to squat, or allows their bottom to stick out backwards (sometimes known as the toilet position!).

THE SNOWPLOUGH TURN

When the skis are being held in a (V) snowplough formation it is easy to see that they are actually pointing in opposite directions. As long as the skier's weight is kept evenly on both skis, they will continue to find the shortest route in a straight line down the slope - the fall line. While sliding forward in this controlled fashion, to commence a turn, either to the right or to the left, it is necessary to apply the above PETS principles to the ski that is already pointing in that direction. That means in order to turn right, the focus must be on the left ski, - remember what we said at the beginning about becoming a completely different animal? This is often a major challenge because it appears initially to contradict human logic. So, for me to begin turning to the right, it means that I need to apply PETS to my left ski.

At this point I must be careful not to lean my body to either side but maintain my dynamic balance by keeping my body position central between my two skis and slightly tipped forward from the waist. My left ski is already on its edge by nature of the snowplough formation (E), I now apply increased pressure (P) and a slight turning of the ski (T) by pressing forward with my left knee against the front of my ski boots so the pressure goes through the big toe on my left foot. Since I am already sliding forward (S) my skis will automatically begin to take me round to the right. As long as I hold this position my skis will continue to turn across the slope until I run out of speed. It is important that there is <u>no other movement or twisting</u> from any other part of my body because this will interfere with the turning process and could destroy my dynamic balance. In these early ski turns there should be absolutely no movement whatsoever in the upper body, all the work is done by the legs through the knees and feet. When I choose to equalise the pressure on the edges of my two skis equally once again, they will immediately begin to turn me back to facing straight downhill. I am now ready to prepare for my next turn.

EARLY STEPS FOR THE CHRISTIAN

In the excitement of beginning to live and move as a Christian and starting to see everything differently, it is easy to get carried away with the new feelings and sensations of living by faith. This means that it is also quite easy to overbalance through a lack of concentration. However, we can discover very quickly that we are now engaged in a battle within our minds. It is a spiritual battle and one in which it is likely to take as much time learning not to do some things, as it is actually learning what we should be doing. Just like developing the ability to execute ski turns, learning how to keep still is a very important quality in the Christian life. In order to be sensitive to the voice of The Lord and to know His guidance, we must learn how to shut out all other distractive influences. The trouble is, wanting to shut them out doesn't mean that they go away. We have to develop the techniques to block them from our minds and then give ourselves time to focus our attention onto Him. In the same way that ski turns are initiated with quite subtle movements rather than grand actions that require huge effort and energy, we need to understand that it is often the subtle changes we make in the way we conduct ourselves as Christians that have the greatest effect, rather than bold, attention-seeking gestures. We must gradually learn how to stand firmly on the promises of God's Word and allow Him to take us forward without leaning heavily in any one direction. We must try not to force the issue or to take back control by bartering with God or using human reasoning, but by simply responding to His promptings. Finally, we must maintain our spiritual dynamic balance by remaining calm and composed at all times, keeping our eyes open to what is around us and staying spiritually alert in every situation regardless of what the circumstances may be telling us.

THE TRAVERSE

Traversing is a way of moving across a ski slope either staying at the same height or moving diagonally down the slope. It involves the skier adopting a stable position by digging the uphill edges of both skis firmly into the snow to allow a smooth journey across the slope while at all times maintaining good dynamic balance. So, for example, when moving across to the right, with both skis parallel and a comfortable distance apart, it is the right-hand edges (the uphill edges) of each ski that create a tiny platform for the skis to slide along and this will hold the skier to prevent any skidding sideways during this manoeuvre. Good edge control is achieved here by firstly holding the uphill (right) ski slightly ahead of the lower ski and then turning the upper body outwards to face downhill, still maintaining good balance. This has the effect of pushing the hips uphill towards the slope, producing an angle on the legs which enables the edges of the skis to be accentuated. Both legs must remain flexed forward at the knees keeping pressure on the toes to absorb any bumps or undulations. With the upper body still tilted slightly forward, stability is maintained by exerting strong pressure on the lower (downhill) ski while keeping the body positioned centrally over both skis at all times.

The most common mistakes people tend to make when learning this skill are:

a) having too much weight on the top (right) ski which then tends to flatten and lose its grip allowing the skier to skid downhill sideways.

b) standing too upright on the skis which allows the hips to drift outwards flattening both skis resulting in a similar loss of control

c) allowing the shoulders to turn to face the direction of travel which allows the hips to drift out.

d) leaning in towards the slope so the body position is no longer central between both skis and the grip of the lower ski is lost.

SPIRITUAL TRAVERSING

Conducting ourselves in a smooth and gentle manner when we encounter all kinds of situations and circumstances is a type of Christian traversing. We can make good progress across all kinds of terrain when we stay flexible yet continue to hold our shape by not compromising. Staying flexible means that we are able to avoid the temptation to become dogmatic in our views. We can do this by riding the criticisms and knockbacks rather than fighting them and we are able to do this by maintaining a strong spiritual posture. A strong posture means that we need to be confident and secure about who we are in Christ Jesus, recognise where we have come from, and know where we are going - in Him. We have been made new in Him, He has brought us out of darkness and into His glorious light, we are children of the living God, born again into His spiritual family, heirs of God (Romans 8 v 16 -17) and destined for an eternity with Him (1 John 5 v 13). Having this kind of security enables us to be flexible in the way we relate to others. Flexibility in this context means that we remain humble in spirit - remembering that we are sinners saved only by His grace

– so that we don't become hard, rigid or judgemental in our views. That would increase the likelihood of us being easily knocked off balance by silly little obstacles. Jesus demonstrated this balance between total security and complete humility when He chose to wash the feet of the disciples – John 13 v 3. This is another example of the importance of holding in balance what appear to be two opposing principles. If we focus on either our strength or our flexibility to the exclusion of the other, we would be making

9. The Stem Christie provides an excellent way of transitioning from snowplough turns into parallel turn

a serious mistake that is likely to take us down a path towards falling into error. So, we learn to hold both of these principles in their entirety without losing the essence of either, now that requires maturity.

THE STEM CHRISTIANIA

This ski turn was developed in Norway by ski jumper Sondre Norheim around 1850 and was given the name of the then capital of Norway, Christiania. Later, the title was shortened and became known as the 'Stem Christie'. It is a useful way of facilitating a turn across the ski slope from traversing in one direction to traversing in the other direction by building on the skills learned in doing snowplough turns. It is based on the principle of stepping out, or stemming, the upper ski from the parallel traversing position into a snowplough formation. That ski then remains as the outside ski of the turn until the skier is facing the new direction when the inner ski (now the upper ski) is brought parallel to form the new traversing position. It provides a useful mid-stage in the development from snowplough turns into parallel turns because it can be mastered at fairly slow speeds without sacrificing dynamic balance.

The turn begins with the skis moving along in the traverse formation where both skis are on their uphill edges and the skier is holding more pressure on the downhill (lower) ski. To commence the turn, the skier stems out the upper ski, changing it from its upper (outside) edge onto its downhill (inside) edge, and into a traditional snowplough formation. It is important at this stage for skiers to keep their centre of gravity centrally between both skis but begin to exert more pressure in the centre of the stemmed out ski by pressing firmly forward with the knee and down onto the ball of the foot. Good body posture and core body weight are kept central between the feet, which maintains dynamic balance, whilst the PETS principles are applied to the outer ski by the leverage of the lower leg. As the turn is progressing the outer ski of the turn becomes the downhill (lower) ski of the new direction so, while pressure is still being exerted on this ski, the inside ski of the turn (now the upper ski) is gently turned and slid-in until it is parallel with the lower ski. This sliding-in of the top ski is done by 'rolling the knee and twisting the ski'. Whilst still keeping some pressure on the toes of this foot, the knee is rolled outwards to change the edge of the ski and the foot is twisted round allowing the ski to slide into parallel. This turn is effected most efficiently when there is absolutely no movement of the upper body so that good dynamic balance is maintained throughout. The upper body of the skier should remain facing squarely downhill throughout the turn so that all the movement comes only from the legs.

A STEP TOWARDS MATURITY

The Stem Christie provides an illustration of how the Christian can begin to make progress towards spiritual maturity. It will inevitably involve taking some steps in a new direction while, at the same time, keeping a strong and immovable body core. The ski turn works best when the skier is moving forward in the traverse at a reasonable speed so that the stemmed-out ski begins to bite as soon as pressure is put on it. The best examples of Christians growing in their faith always occur when they are actively going on in their relationship with The Lord and not when they are static. God makes His promises freely available to us but, in order to receive them, it requires us to be living for Him and then to make a conscious choice to step into them. There will usually be an element of fear and trepidation attached to any opportunity to move into an area that is outside our existing experience, but growth and development only happen when we agree to something changing. Someone once defined a miracle as 'Doing what you've always done but expecting a different outcome'. We must learn how to make important changes in our lifestyle if we are to grow towards maturity.

To even attempt to keep our Christian faith static is a contradiction in terms. The Bible explains that we are on a journey and although our final destination is clear, we have a lot to learn along the way. It is a constantly changing relationship in which The Lord is trying to encourage us to move and grow every day. Here is another of those diametrically opposed Biblical principles that we must hold in balance: we must constantly be willing to change, yet some things must be absolutely unchangeable and immovable. I have known Christians who have been tempted to be constantly changing by chasing every new idea or innovation and consequently have experienced no real stability in their faith. They are often perceived by others as 'flakey'. I have known other Christians who became so set in their ways that they found it impossible to change and eventually lost their sense of God's presence and peace. They are often perceived by others as being miserable and out of date. I believe there are two main aspects for us to be aware of here: a) we must have an unshakeable confidence in The Bible as the inspired Word of God and be committed to studying and exploring it as much as we possibly can, and b) we must spend time every day in direct two-way communication with The Lord so that we become sensitive to the gentle promptings of His Holy Spirit and become willing to respond immediately to whatever He asks of us. (see the Gateway to Life Booklet – 'Moving Forward' which sets out 7 key principles for spiritual growth). It is only as we maintain a stable core strength that we will be confident about stepping boldly into the new things God has for us.

GOING PARALLEL

The transition from a Stem Christie to a parallel turn can be accomplished by blending the movements together at a slightly faster speed. It can be helpful at first, to practise doing the turns very closely together while descending in as straight a line as possible down a gentle slope. As a person's confidence grows they are able to allow their speed to increase and this makes it easier to eliminate all movement from the upper body throughout each turn and to smoothly slide each ski into its new position without lifting it from the surface. Moving at a slightly faster pace can also help to maintain dynamic balance and keep the core body weight central while the legs are being pushed out to apply the PETS principles onto the outer ski of each turn. To begin with, you will feel the resistance under the outer ski in each turn as you push it away from you and then steer the other ski parallel. Gradually these movements begin to flow together smoothly so that instead of turning each ski independently by rotating each leg separately, you naturally begin to turn, change the edges and exert pressure on both skis at the same time - this is a parallel turn. Once the principle of keeping the skis parallel in the turn has been mastered, it needs to be refined and developed so that the radius of the turns can be adjusted and modified at different speeds, on different gradients and in different snow conditions. Our turns will continue to improve as we get better at absorbing all the bumps and hollows with our legs by using the flexibility in our ankles and knees. This then, enables us to keep our upper body quiet, keep our eyes focused on the terrain ahead, and maintain good dynamic balance.

UNWEIGHTING

The smoothness in the parallel turns is eventually made possible by an action called 'unweighting'. This enables an immediate reduction in the pressure on both skis at the same moment and makes it possible for both skis to be turned simultaneously by rotating the legs. At this point, the edges of both skis are changed at the same time before the downward pressure returns to make the new edges bite and facilitate the turn. Unweighting can be achieved either by a quick extension of the legs creating an upward movement of the whole body, or a sudden compression of the legs by lifting the knees towards the torso. These actions momentarily take the weight off the skis so that they can be easily realigned to commence the new turn. Here again, it is important that all the movement comes from the legs so that the upper body can remain quietly in dynamic balance at all times.

When beginning to develop this technique, it is quite difficult to keep it smooth and it is common for the action to be jerky and over emphasised. The skill develops as the person becomes more aware of how these movements are affecting the contact their skis have with the snow and this, with practice, enables them to make their actions softer and smoother.

SMOOTH CHRISTIANITY

Most new Christians find that beginning to walk by faith can be quite an effort in the early days and that over emphasising our faith can actually create as many problems as not exercising our faith at all. Learning to trust

God in everything and be sensitive to His voice can be a struggle because it seems so much easier to simply carry on doing what we've done in the past. The disciplines of spending time in prayer and reading The Bible can appear to be an unnecessary pressure because it just seems to take valuable time out of our day. It is only as we make these disciplines a priority by continuing to practise them every day that they will begin to become an indispensable part of our life. Our days will only begin to flow smoothly, regardless of the circumstances we may be facing, when we see these disciplines as absolutely essential. Jesus demonstrated the importance of this principle to His disciples when He calmed the storm on lake Galilee (Luke 8 v 22 – 25).

Generally we tend to ask Jesus to protect us from the storms of life by bringing calmness and peace all around us. Sometimes He does this, however, instead of this, He will often produce calmness and peace on the inside of us so that we are better able to handle the storm that continues to rage on the outside, yet not be fazed by it. The peace that God makes available to us is not just the absence of external turmoil but a deep inner sense of His presence. Jesus made it clear that what He offers is quite different to that which the world offers and this is beyond our ability to understand logically (John 14 v 27). However, it is a quality that the world is desperate to receive. Many who profess a faith in Jesus are never-the-less still battling with issues such as fears, phobias, anxieties and depressions and feel unable to receive His peace. The effort this takes, just to keep going every day, is demoralising as well as emotionally, physically, mentally and spiritually draining. There really is an answer. Please send for my Gateway to Life booklet 'Breaking Free' to discover a way to recover your core stability by dealing with whatever blockages are preventing you from moving on towards spiritual maturity.

Christian Parallels | PART 9

Getting the Best Instruction Possible

We generally don't get much choice when it comes to picking a ski instructor. We will usually be put into a group of people according to our level of ski ability and experience and then allocated a ski instructor by the head of the local ski school in the resort where we are at the time. For lots of people, it can then take some time to begin to get used to the instructor; the inflections of his voice, his accent, his mannerisms and his sense of humour (or not), can all be difficult to master at the start. It is also quite challenging to begin to put your life and safety into the hands of someone you have just met and really know very little about whilst in the company of people you also may not know, in a potentially harsh environment.

There are challenges too to being in a group of people who may react differently to the instructor. Some may be able to rise to the occasion and respond immediately to his demands whereas others may feel threatened, afraid, or out of their depth very quickly. Some may wish to be pushed harder in their learning and others may feel that he is going too fast for them. Such emotional responses for each person will determine whether the learning experience is constructive, exciting and invigorating, or negative, fearful and distressing.

RECOGNISING HOW PEOPLE LEARN

Many years ago while I was instructing in the Alps, a party of people arrived from a small town in South Wales. They were a large group of friends from their local leisure centre and included a mixture of tennis players, squash players, badminton players, athletes, gymnasts, footballers and rugby players along with their partners and children. Many of them had skied before, but I was asked to take on a group of 'first-timers' which was made up predominantly of gymnasts and rugby players. After taking them through the basic ski familiarisation processes, I wanted, as soon as possible, to get them sliding down a gentle slope in a very safe area where they could come to no harm so that they could quickly experience the thrill of being able to ski. I was absolutely amazed to notice that some of the toughest, strongest and fittest guys in the group, who were rugby players, became quite fearful and found their legs turning to jelly while some of the most frail looking guys were becoming extremely animated and were able to throw themselves into their new challenge with great excitement.

This was a real life example which demonstrated clearly that learning to ski has absolutely nothing to do with physical strength or ability but is totally dependent upon a person's mental approach and their willingness to step outside their comfort zone. A ski instructor, therefore, must be someone who is able to recognise that every difficulty in learning to ski is rooted in the person's subconscious and not in their behavioural or physical (or verbal) responses. Of course, it must also be understood that using muscles in a way that a person is not accustomed to doing will always be physically exhausting and so appropriate physical preparation and exercise will be a great help here. However, actually learning to be a skier relies entirely on a person's mental approach.

THE EXEMPLARY SKI INSTRUCTOR

In order to progress most effectively as a skier we need to have an instructor who is in every way our Example, our Guide, and our Teacher. We want to be able to have total faith and trust in this person and to have confidence that he will protect us and provide what we need by being aware of how we are struggling to cope at every stage. We want someone who is able to identify with what we are going through as we seek to face the new challenges that learning new skills in a strange environment will inevitably present to us. We need someone who is able to come down to our level and to speak to us in language we can understand and who will help us draw on the resources we already possess so that we feel encouraged to keep going.

We do not need someone who simply gives us instructions to follow or who demonstrates his own flawless technique without breaking it down for us into easily understandable steps. We have no need of a showy expert who is out of touch with the difficulties we are encountering but one who shows us amazing amounts of patience whenever we get things wrong or make the same mistakes time after time.

Our instructor needs to kind, yet firm, he needs to be consistent, yet flexible, he needs to be able to accept our weaknesses, yet be confident in our ability to progress eventually onto greater things.

OUR CHRISTIAN INSTRUCTOR

Just as in skiing, there is no shortage of people who will want to give us advice and tell us what we should be doing in order to progress in the Christian faith. Some of these will be good and helpful but some will be not so good and could restrict our development by getting us stuck in some of their bad habits. In reality, we have only one instructor, and that is Jesus. He is the only one who understands exactly what we are going through at each stage of our development and he is the only one who is able to provide exactly what we need at each stage. He alone can identify with our struggles and conflicts, He alone understands our worries and fears, He alone can empathise with our questions and doubts, and He alone has absolute confidence in our ability to grow into spiritually mature ambassadors of The Kingdom.

Jesus never pushes us beyond what we are able to manage at any time, yet He never loses His desire to help us develop into new levels of relationship and experience in our faith. He never simply sees us as we are now, or looks only at our external appearance. He is never fazed by our failures or our falls because He looks at our heart and sees us as He originally intended us to be. He is able to use every situation, every challenge and every obstacle that comes across our path as a creative opportunity to develop us more and more into His own likeness. All that He requires of us is our willingness to be completely surrendered to His wisdom and guidance and to put ourselves unreservedly into His hands.

THE INSTRUCTION MANUAL

Lots of enthusiastic skiers choose to purchase a Ski Instruction Manual for themselves so that they can analyse their own performance, detect any weaknesses or errors in their technique, and try to rectify these on their next ski run. Skiers have been known to study a manual like this in the evenings after a day on the slopes, so they can approach the next day with a determination to do better. They will often be discussing the details with their friends and family long into the night and practising how to get the correct body positions whilst in the comfort of their ski chalet. As they pour over the diagrams and descriptions of the ski movements it is almost as though, echoing through the pages, they can hear the words of their ski instructor urging them to do what he is saying.

As we seek to move and grow in the Christian life, we not only have the perfect instructor, but we have the perfect instruction manual, and this is freely available to us at all times – The Holy Bible. Within its pages we have everything explained to us about how to conduct ourselves in order to successfully conquer the harsh environment in which we live so that we will be able to grow into maturity. It gives us stories, illustrations and instructions about all kinds of situations and circumstances that we might have to face and it shows us how to apply these principles in our daily life. As we study this manual for life, it is as though we hear the very words of God speaking to us directly through its pages. It is the most incredible resource and is the only true way of getting to understand our instructor.

Christian Parallels | PART 10

The Role of Competition

In every area of sport and business there seems to be constant pressure on people to strive for improvement. Boundaries are always being pushed back, standards are being raised, and the desire to produce more and do it more quickly is a major driving force in the world today. Many people believe one of the ways to achieve this is by encouraging strong competition. The idea is that it will keep everyone on their toes, not allow people to relax too much but keep their focus on continually trying to develop new ways of making progress. Life is full of challenges and if we can see these in a positive light, they will encourage us to be better, stronger and more skilful at whatever we choose to do. Many people think the Christian life is only for wimps but the reality is that you will face many more challenges if you try to live as a Christian than you will by deciding not to bother. God explains, in The Bible, that He allows us to be challenged, and even brings challenges into our lives, so that we might become stronger in our faith (1 Peter 5 v 10).

THE CHALLENGE

Therefore it is necessary for us to appreciate the importance of being pushed beyond what we think we are capable of achieving, even though this will usually require us to go through the pain barrier. The pain barrier is that point at which we would normally stop or give up what we are doing because it hurts. Generally speaking, great things will only be accomplished by those who choose to push through, in spite of the pain and discomfort. The best example of this is the 'body-builder' – someone who is working to build up their muscles by lifting weights. As the pain of exertion begins to bite, they grit their teeth and push on to do one or two extra repetitions of the exercise. The pain is caused by the muscles actually breaking down so that the blood which flows through their arteries and veins can re-build the muscles stronger that they were before. To do this requires some serious motivation, and one of the strongest motivators

10. Slalom races are a great way to improve a skier's skill, flexibility and speed of reactions.

is the challenge of competition. This is what creates the necessity for dedication and commitment to some tough training schedules. Every person has an in-built desire to want to be better - at something and, in so many spheres of life competition is a way of comparing our progress with others in order to demonstrate whether it is working.

In skiing, many different competitions have been developed in recent years which make the sport more attractive and entertaining and which push the boundaries of those who wish to compete. This, then, drives the development of better clothing and equipment, demands the creation of better and more challenging facilities, increases the exposure of the sport, which then attracts more sponsorship. All this contributes to raising the levels of excitement and expectation of the public at large. This presents a challenge to ski areas to improve their access and accommodation, to create more ski runs, install more ski lifts, build better restaurants, cafes and 'apres-ski' facilities. Holiday companies then want to offer better deals to more ski resorts and so on. Competition, therefore, in all its forms, plays an essential part in the on-going growth of the whole skiing industry world-wide.

IS THERE COMPETITION IN CHRISTIANITY ?

For the Christian faith, there are three massive areas where we experience a serious sense of competition (there may be others too). The first, is the hundreds of religions, cults, beliefs and traditions that are contrary to the Christian faith and which continue to ensnare people every day. The second is the intense human desire we all possess to try to prove that we can be independent of God. The third is the work of the devil. Each of these areas create an aspect of competition in our hearts and minds which causes a real battle between our old unregenerate nature and our new nature, which God is fashioning into a greater likeness of Himself. Whenever we come face to face with issues like this we are likely to be challenged about our knowledge of The Word and the level of our dedication and commitment to The Lord. God's desire in this is to motivate us to improve these elements of our faith and grow towards a stronger sense of maturity in Him (Ephesians 4 v 14-15). God never wants any challenge to weaken us, but always to strengthen us and draw us closer to Him. However, He loves us so much that He doesn't want us simply to stay as we are. He always has better things for us because He is preparing us for our role with Him in eternity.

i. Other religions etc.
    The competition in which we are engaged with other religions and cults is to demonstrate the truth and resist the temptation to distort or disbelieve the Word of God. Do we really know what The Bible says about what others are choosing to believe? If we were demonstrating the true power of the living Lord Jesus in our lives on a daily basis, as we should, people would see this and be challenged to explore it for themselves. It is an indictment upon us that so few non-Christian people feel challenged in this way. Many religious approaches appear to offer solutions to the needs people are experiencing and so seem to be attractive at the time. A friend of mine who was a Jehovah's Witness once told me that up to 95% of their adherents are people who received a visit from a Witness at a time when they were going through a period of crisis and then responded to the companionship, help and support that was being offered at that time.
    We all have a spiritual dimension within which our deep core needs for security, significance and self-worth have to be met. Therefore people are tempted to latch onto whatever may be available to them at the time and, for many, that will be some form of religious connection. Unfortunately, every religious connection that is not firmly based on The Bible will tend to lead people away from God and will not therefore be able to fully satisfy these core needs. The challenge for us here is to demonstrate that there is only one way to be certain of knowing a level of security, significance and self-worth that can never be shaken.

ii.   Human drive for independence.

One of the most destructive qualities that human beings possess is the intense desire we all have to demonstrate our independence from God. It will tend to surface for us in different ways and at different times but no-one is immune from it and it can lead us into making some really bad decisions.   Our attempts to prove ourselves will always lead us further and further away from God and will often make it much more difficult for us to learn to trust Him.   This drive is often completely sub-conscious so we can easily convince ourselves that our decisions are perfectly logical, appropriate and genuinely in our own best interests.   We find it comparatively easy to make choices according the knowledge and experience we have acquired in life and this produces for us a real sense of self-satisfaction and self-fulfilment. Generally, one of three main opinions come into play here; as long as we are convinced that God doesn't exist, we won't feel guilty about not trusting Him, if we believe He does exist, then we can convince ourselves that He doesn't care about us sufficiently to be really interested in the decisions we want to make or, we may get so caught up by the physical world around us that we simply overlook the spiritual, and forget to consult The Lord. Whatever the case may be, the result is that we have an inherent drive to prove that we are perfectly capable of managing our lives successfully without God. The real dilemma here is that unless we learn to surrender ourselves completely to Him, we will never find the satisfaction and fulfilment we crave. We get caught up on a treadmill of believing what the world tells us - that if we work harder and are more sincere, we will eventually achieve satisfaction in this life, but this is a road that leads to exhaustion, burnout, stress and depression. For the Christian, we must realise that although hard work and using our skills constructively may produce many benefits, we must never allow these to become a substitute for making God the number one priority in our lives. This is an internal battle we cannot win as long as we continue to justify such actions in our own minds.

iii.   The work of the devil.

Whether we believe it or not, the devil is a real person who is intent on preventing us from receiving everything God has made available to us (1 Peter 5 v 8). His strategy is to tempt us, accuse us, trick us, inflict us, rob us and oppress us in every way possible so that we will be distracted from choosing to put our trust in God. One of his biggest weapons is 'doubt'. He tries to cast doubt onto everything we believe in order to make us question its validity. This, in turn, makes us uncertain and unstable in our faith (Genesis 3 v 1) and susceptible to following popular opinion. There is nothing wrong with experiencing doubt, nor of raising difficult questions. The challenge here, is that what we do with them and how we handle them will determine whether we grow weaker or stronger. If we face our doubts, and own up to them, we are able to search for the truth and find answers to our questions that are based on fact rather than fable. We are able to invite God's Holy Spirit to lead us (John 16 v 13) into a better understanding of the person of Jesus, who is Truth (John 14 v 6). Therefore, if we rise to the occasion, we have the ability to see every obstacle or difficulty as an opportunity for us to grow stronger and every setback as a springboard to reaching new heights in our relationship with The Lord.

Whatever forms of temptation we may face can be handled best by reminding ourselves of the truths of The Bible, but in order for this to be effective, we must be clear about what God has actually said in the Scriptures (Genesis 3 v 3) and not rely on what someone else has told us.

Learning how we might best be able to benefit from these elements of competition is a sign of growing maturity. For the Christian, there are no winners or losers in the traditional sense of competition, but only in terms of the outcome. It is a clear principle throughout The Bible that God chooses to regularly bring challenges into our lives because His plan is to build us into the people He originally designed us to be. So every time we give in to a challenge – we miss out on the ways He wants to bless us, and every time we fail to learn from a challenge – we miss also out. Initially this means that we will tend to stagnate in our spiritual growth. Over time, this means that we will begin to feel less connected to God, less able to call out to Him for help, more lethargic and more isolated. We actually need to be jolted back into a competitive mindset where we are reminded that through every situation God's unchanging love only wants to make us stronger and more effective for Him and that He can turn every problem or disaster and every crisis or trial into something of spiritual benefit for us.

Christian Parallels | PART 11

Fearless Sensitivity

O nce we begin to grow towards maturity in the Christian life, God will constantly want to introduce new things that will change us to become more and more like Him (2 Corinthians 3 v 18). However, one of the most amazing things about the way God changes us is that He doesn't remove any of the gifts, skills, abilities or talents with which He has endowed us. What He does, though, is transform what He has already given us by anointing us with His supernatural power so that whatever we surrender to Him becomes more beautiful, more useful, more powerful and more effective for the work of building the kingdom of God.

Before the apostle Peter met Jesus he was, in every sense, a rough diamond. He was a hardened fisherman, used to working in all weathers often under very difficult circumstances. He was outspoken, impetuous and wasn't fazed by anything or anybody. It took 3 years of living alongside Jesus to polish this diamond, during which time he also learned sensitivity but, like most people, he appeared to confuse sensitivity with weakness. When he was challenged after the crucifixion of Jesus, he was afraid, denied his association with Jesus, and ran away, only meeting with the other disciples in secret. It wasn't until 7 weeks later, on the day of Pentecost, when the supernatural Holy Spirit descended upon the disciples in power, that God banished his fear and anointed his bold outspokenness so that it turned him into a powerful and sensitive ambassador for the Kingdom.

EACH IS MADE COMPLETE BY THE OTHER

So often people may be able to demonstrate one or other of the qualities of fearlessness and sensitivity, but it is rare to discover a person who is able to demonstrate both. To the inexperienced person they appear to be opposing principles, but to the mature person they are an essential combination. As people move towards a greater level of maturity it becomes more important to be able to demonstrate both of these qualities. Many people fail to progress into maturity because they put too great an emphasis on either one of these to the detriment of the other. Fearlessness, if not tempered by sensitivity, can produce an over-confident brashness which can be interpreted as being big-headed, pushy, or arrogant. Sensitivity, if not complemented by fearlessness, can appear in the form of reticence, withdrawal or extreme shyness. Now we need to look at each of these attributes not just from a physical perspective, but consider them when they are wholly surrendered to The Lord and anointed with His Holy Spirit. It is then, when the spiritual quality of both of these elements are working together that they are able to produce a strength in us which has supernatural qualities because it is like Jesus living through us.

BOLDNESS WITH BALANCE

We can witness the purely physical aspects of this principle when we watch competent skiers coping with the changes in snow conditions and gradients on a bumpy 'black' ski run. Their boldness, strength and confidence comes from having previously developed the skills necessary to face such a challenge but this needs to be combined with a sensitivity to 'feel' the surface through their feet, along with great flexibility in their legs in order to maintain their dynamic balance. Put together, these qualities allow the skier to respond instantly to any changes in the surface of the snow whilst appearing totally calm and unruffled the whole time.

From a Christian point of view, this is what we refer to as Spiritual Maturity. It is the ability to successfully navigate our way through difficult and dangerous circumstances without being fazed by them. The fearlessness comes through our total faith and unreserved commitment to our Almighty Heavenly Father. Through this we can experience the reality of His presence within us which enables us to know that He, like His Word, is unchangeable and unshakeable. Consequently we have a boldness to face any obstacle that may come across our path, regardless of its origin, because we are surrendered to the One in whom is all power and all authority. The sensitivity comes from keeping our spiritual feet on the ground. We achieve this by walking and talking with The Lord every day so that we know how to recognise His voice and have learned how to respond to Him through our obedience to whatever He asks of us. In this close relationship we learn to recognise the softness of His touch in our lives and will have heard the gentle whisperings of His Holy Spirit. We will have witnessed His healing power which brings release from oppression creating a lightness in our spirit and we will have known the in-filling of His Holy Spirit who brings to us a supernatural balance and poise in everything we do.

HUMILITY

As skiers, we must realise that we can never control the mountain, or the weather, but we are like guests – privileged, for a time, to be allowed to enjoy the beautiful environment in which we find ourselves. Therefore we get excited about wanting to get the very best out of our time without ever losing our respect or sense of awe for our surroundings. So, within these limitations, full enjoyment for us will always mean that we retain our child-like ability to be totally engrossed and fully abandoned to our skiing. Such a level of fulfilment is made possible by knowing that our core needs of Security, Significance and Self-Worth are being catered for, at least to some extent, by the level of skills we have learned and the quality of the equipment we are using. For the Christian, Security, Significance and Self-Worth come not from our knowledge and experience of life, but from our relationship with Jesus and by knowing that our Heavenly Father is in ultimate control. As we surrender our lives to Him we allow His presence to fill us and His power to work through us. This principle is summed up most beautifully in the words of this hymn:

Father I place into your hands the things I cannot do
Father I place into your hands the things that I've been through
Father I place into your hands the way that I should go
For I know I always can trust you.

Father I place into your hands my friends and family
Father I place into your hands the things that trouble me
Father I place into your hands the person I would be
For I know I always can trust you.

Father I love to see your face, I love to hear your voice
Father I love to sing your praise and in your name rejoice
Father I love to walk with you and in your presence rest
For I know I always can trust you

Father I want to be with you and do the things you do
Father I want to speak the words that you are speaking too
Father I want to love the ones that you will draw to you
For I know that I am one with you

Author: Jenny Hewer (1975) Thank You Music

Christian maturity, therefore, is understanding and applying the specific balance between allowing God to work out His purposes in our lives, and using the gifts and skills He has already given us to do things in our own strength. Trying to resolve things ourselves by taking things into our own hands, however talented we may be, is a sign of immaturity.

NOT GETTING OFF BALANCE

One big mistake that is often made in Christian circles, is for people to spend time pleading with God to do what He has actually asked us to do and to end up doing the things that He has said He will do. In this way we so easily get the balance wrong in our relationship with Him and then cannot understand why things don't seem to work out for us as we desire. For example, we can ask God to send revival into our community yet not be willing to be the vehicles through whom He will make it happen. Then again, we often think it is our job to convince people of their sin when actually it is the work of The Holy Spirit. It is so easy for us to get unbalanced in our faith that it can happen almost without our realising it. How many times have you heard someone beseeching The Lord to come into a meeting, or praying earnestly for Him to show up, or inviting The Holy Spirit to come into the room? I tend to think that such a person either hasn't read The Book or simply doesn't believe it (see Psalm 139 v 7 - 10). When we fall into this trap, we are demonstrating that we are still exercising the mentality of the world which says "If I don't see it, I won't believe it", and consequently faith gets squeezed out. It is absolutely essential for us to develop an unshakable trust in what God has said in the Scriptures, otherwise we will never be able to live powerfully and fearlessly for Him and we will always be struggling to stay upright, in a spiritual sense.

CHRISTIAN MATURITY

Christian maturity speaks about the quality of being able to handle difficult situations with a smoothness that belies the seriousness of the issues. It is being unfazed by the physical evidence of the circumstances around us because we have greater faith in a higher power - that of our creator. It is the knowledge and wisdom of how to use our talents and abilities to the best advantage for God, whilst not dismissing our weaknesses, and by keeping ourselves in subjection to The Lord at all times. It is knowing the difference between taking on something because we think we can do it, as opposed to taking on something because God has asked us to do it - even if we feel we can't do it. The delicate balance needed here can only be achieved once we have learned how to distinguish the voice of God from the myriad of other voices we may hear, and then learned to be courageous in our willingness to be obedient to Him regardless of what our physical senses are telling us.

The Christian, just like the skier, is going to encounter different challenges every day and so maturity must be a constantly developing quality. It is not something that once acquired, remains static or permanent, but instead requires constant attention and spiritual growth to continue to be relevant. What may have seemed a mature response yesterday may not be relevant at all today. So we need to be careful not to fall into using the same approaches, techniques or words that may have worked in the past. This leads towards a ritualistic approach and shows a distinct lack of maturity. There is no formula in Christian maturity, it is all about our personal relationship with Jesus. We must be able to rejoice constantly in the certainty that God's mercies are new every morning and, as a result, allow praise and worship to flow spontaneously out of our hearts.

About the Author

Trevor Summerlin has, for over 30 years been the Principal of **Positive Release**, an organisation dedicated to the very highest standards of Counselling, Psychotherapy, Training, Supervision and Coaching based on tried, tested and proven Christian principles.

Prior to this, Trevor spent over 20 years working in Outdoor Activities and qualified as a BASI ski instructor and an England Ski Council Coach.

He had experience in senior management and marketing around the world, before being called into the Ministry as a Baptist Pastor. Here he established a Registered Charity, formed a Limited Company, opened a community shop, and an alcohol-free bar working with hundreds of teenagers every week.

He has also qualified as a Youth Worker and Trainer, as a Family Law Mediator, as a Cognitive Behavioural Psychotherapist, and as a Professional Coach. He is a Fellow of the Institute of Sales and Marketing Management (now known as Institute of Sales Management), a Fellow of the Institute of Leadership and Management and a member of the British Association for Counselling and Psychotherapy since 1996.

His on-going passion is to help people understand that by applying the principles of The Bible everyday in their lives, they will give themselves the very best chance of being successful at whatever they choose to do.

Trevor and his wife Jan (ex Nurse and Counsellor), are based in Abergavenny, South Wales, where they are kept busy with Bible teaching, Christian Counselling, Writing and managing their garden.

The Gateway to Life Programme

The Gateway to Life is a series of small booklets aimed at helping people explore various aspects of the Christian faith on the journey towards spiritual maturity.

Each booklet should be a shared journey towards developing a better understanding of the topic and is designed be undertaken by a small group of people, or a family.

GtL No. 1-   The Fundamentals (Green)
This is a very basic introduction to Christianity. It looks at 4 of the fundamental issues on which our faith is based.

GtL No.2 -   Moving Forward (Blue)
This identifies 7 foundational elements of the Christian faith which are essential for people wishing to grow and move towards spiritual maturity.

GtL No. 3 -   Breaking Free (Red)
This gives people a strategy of 3 things to explore, then 5 steps to take to identify and deal with any issues that may be blocking their spiritual growth.

GtL No. 4 -   Understanding The Holy Spirit (White)
This aims to give understanding of Holy Spirit by considering His 3 distinct roles and then answering some of the major concerns that frequently arise.

GtL No. 5 – Exploring Worship (Orange)
This helps people explore the wider concepts of developing a worshipping lifestyle by looking at 5 key elements.

GtL No. 6 – Christian Paradoxes (Pink)
This looks at some of the controversial issues that could hinder a person's development towards Spiritual Maturity.

GtL No. 7 – Spiritual Maturity (Purple)
Here we consider some of the behaviours that lead towards Spiritual Maturity and the characteristics that will be evident when demonstrating it.

Series produced by **Positive Release,**
Abergavenny, Monmouthshire, WALES, UK
saltandlight@btinternet.com

For more details, see **www.gateway-to-life.programme**

Lightning Source UK Ltd.
Milton Keynes UK
UKHW050754110722
405653UK00005B/3